LLC

Quick Start Beginner's Guide To Limited Liability Companies

Chris Cohen & Gabriel Fischer

© 2016 Copyright.

Text copyright reserved by
Chris Cohen & Gabriel Fischer

The contents of this book may not be reproduced, duplicated or transmitted without direct written permission from the authors

Disclaimer : all attempts have been made by the author to provide factual and accurate content. No responsibility will be taken by the author for any damages caused by misuse of the content described in this book. The content of this book has been derived from various sources. Please consult a licensed professional before attempting any techniques outlined in this book.

Table of Contents

Introduction

Chapter 1 - Overview

Chapter 2 - How to Raise Capital to Start an LLC

Chapter 3 – Benefits

Chapter 4 - 10 Things to Avoid

Chapter 5 - Giving Your Limited Liability Company a Great Name

Chapter 6 - Reviewing Tax Types for Limited Liability Companies

Chapter 7 – Accounting and Bookkeeping

Chapter 8 – Recap: Why operate as an LLC?

Chapter 9 – Step by Step Guide On How to Create a Limited Liability Company

Chapter 10 – The Responsibilities and Rights as Member of an LLC

Chapter 11 – Dissolving an LLC

Chapter 12 – Why You Can Be Forced to Wind Up Your LLC

Chapter 13 – The Much You Need to Know About LLC Bankruptcy

Conclusion

Introduction

Limited liability companies are the go-to form of incorporating for those who would like to start a company without having to worry about their personal assets being repossessed if they fail to pay their creditors. It's also a great form of protection for those who don't want to end up having to open up their company to the public. While limited liabilities can be opened to the public if the company needs funding, they can remain closed so that only the partners of the company are able to hold stocks in the company.

It's important to understand that a limited liability company does not protect its owners and operators from all forms of debt collection and judgments. There are some scenarios where the owners and managers of the company will have to answer to the creditors and the law, but those will be described later on in this book.

If you're the owner of a small company that would like to bring in partners or would just like the protection a limited liability company offers, then keep reading to find out how incorporating can help you!

Chapter 1 - Overview

If you haven't already explored what a Limited Liability Company is, then let's go over what they are briefly in this chapter.

Just as a shareholder of a corporation, the limited liability company owners are exempt from personal liability for business claims and debts. This means that if they business is not able to pay someone they owe like a lender, supplier, or a landlord, then the person they owe is not able to come after them directly for their house, car, or personal possessions. Because only the company's assets are used to pay off a business debt, the owners will only lose the money they invested in the company. This feature is known as limited liability.

However, there are some exceptions to limited liability companies. They are not something to protect the owners of the company from everything, just financial responsibilities to creditors. Some things owners of limited liability companies are still responsible for include personally or directly injuring another person, personally guaranteeing a business loan or a bank loan where the company defaults, failing to despot taxes withheld from the employee's wages, intentionally doing something illegal or fraudulent that causes harm to the company or someone else, or treating the company as an extension of their personal affairs rather than a separate entity.

The last exception mentioned is perhaps the most important out of them all. If an owner doesn't treat the business as if it were a separate entity, the court can decide that limited liability does not exist and find the owners are actually doing business as individuals who are personally liable for their actions. To keep this from happening, you can do a few things.

The first thing is to act fairly and legally. Don't misinterpret or conceal material facts or the state of the finances to creditors, vendors, or outsiders. Fund the company properly. Invest enough cash in the business so that it's able to meet foreseeable expenses. Keep the company and personal business separate. Get a separate federal employer identification number for the business, open up a checking account for the business, and keep personal finances and the business finances separate. Lastly, create an operating agreement. Having a formal written operating agreement gives the company credibility and a separate existence.

Another mistake most that open up a limited liability make is that they don't purchase additional protection in the form of business insurance. Liability insurance will keep the owner of the company shielded from their personal assets being repossessed when limited liability is not enough. For example, let's say you're a massage therapist and you injured a client's back by accident. Liability insurance should cover you. Insurance will also protect your personal assets in the event that a court ignores the limited liability status.

In addition to protecting personal assets, insurance will also protect the company's assets from claims and lawsuits. But the company will not be protected if it doesn't pay the bill. Commercial insurance will not usually protect corporate or personal possessions from unpaid business obligations, whether or not they were personally guaranteed.

Types of LLCs

Limited liability companies come in different kinds, which affects how they're taxed. These are:

Single Member: For taxation purposes, this kind of LLC isn't treated as a separate, juridical entity from its member. What this means is that the LLC's income is reported under the income of its member for purposes of filing tax returns.

Multiple Member: This kind of LLC obviously has more than a single member and that isn't the only difference between the two. A multi-member LLC is considered a separate juridical entity in terms of filing taxes. This simply means that unlike single member LLCs, its members can benefit through passing through of losses and profits pretty much the way partners do in business partnerships.

Non-Profit: This type of LLC enjoys practically the same advantages in terms of taxation as non-profit corporations. Plus, it's also as flexible as partnerships but when it comes to liabilities, its members are as protected as the owners of profit corporations. However, non-profit LLCs aren't allowed in all states in the US.

Professional: This kind of LLC – also referred to as PLLCs for brevity, is a company with limited liabilities, which are organized solely for providing professional services such as medical and legal, among others.

Series: This kind of LLC (SLLC) is quite a special one. The reason it's special is because as a single LLC, it's allowed to segregate its resources or assets into separate series or sub-LLCs as a way of protecting its resources from potential claims of creditors.

While LLCs are sometimes called limited liability corporations or LLC corporations, it's nothing more than a term of reference and not a legal one because under the law, LLC corporations don't exist, at least in the United States.

Strategic Alliances?

Strategic alliances are agreements between several entities, which are formalized, with the achievement of particular goals and meeting of specific needs that are related to business. These agreements are formalized and during the effectivity of the agreement, each entity in the alliance continues to remain independent of each other. Think of it as some sort of an LLC joint venture.

Management

The LLC's Operating Agreement and Articles of Organization may set the management powers of its managers or members. If the LLC's management is entrusted to managers, they're given the exclusive authority to make decisions and enforce actions that bind the LLC. However, a manager-led LLC may only take action after securing a majority vote, so in that sense, such an LLC is similar to a corporation. On the flip side, the actions or decisions of a member of an LLC that's member-managed may bind the LLC and as such, a member-managed LLC is akin to partnerships.

Legal Assistance

Before deciding on or finalizing your corporate structure, it's essential that you seek legal advice or assistance first, especially if it's your first time to organize an LLC. An attorney who's well-versed and experienced in handling business related matters can give you sound advice on the legal advantages and disadvantages of each type of business structure, be it an LLC, partnership, corporation or a sole proprietorship. Similarly, such lawyers can assist you in drafting the necessary legal and corporate documents, making sure that they're compliant with the laws of the particular state you plan to set up your business.

Taxes

When it comes to taxes, limited liabilities are not considered separate from their owners for tax purposes. Rather, it's what the IRS terms a pass-through entity, just like a sole proprietorship or partnership. This means business income goes through the business to the owners, who then report their share of the profits or losses on their individual income tax returns. Every member of the company has to make a quarterly estimated tax payment to the IRS.

While limited liability companies don't pay taxes themselves, co-owned ones have to file a Form 1065, an informational return, with the IRS every year. This form shows the members' shares of the profits or losses, which the IRS when then review to make sure the members of the company are reporting their income properly.

Management

The owners of almost every small limited liability company participate in an equal manner in the management of the business. This arrangement is also known as member management. There's an alternative structure for management known as manager management, where one or more of the owners or an outsider is designated as responsible for managing the company. The non-managing owners will sit back and share in the profits of the company.

In a manager-managed limited liability company, only the named managers will get a vote on the management decisions and act as agents of the company. Choosing the manager management method will sometimes make sense, but it can require with some state and federal laws that regulate the sales of securities.

Creating an LLC

To make a limited liability company, you have to file a certificate of organization or an article of organization with the limited liability division of the state government. This office is usually in the same division as the corporation's department, which is most likely going to be part of the secretary of state's agency. Filing fees can range anywhere from a hundred to eight hundred dollars. In every state, you are able to form a limited liability company with just one person.

Many states will supply a one-page form for the articles of organization, on which you will only need a few basic details about the company, as the name and address, as well as contact information forth person involved with the company who is known as the registered agent. This is the person who will receive legal documentation on the company's behalf. Some states will also require the list the names and addresses of the members of the company.

As well as filing the articles of organization, the creator of the company must also make a written limited liability corporation operating agreement. That person doesn't have to file the operating agreement with the state, but that doesn't mean they are able to get by without having one. The operating agreement is a crucial document because it sets out the member's rights and responsibilities, their percent of interests in the business, and their share of the profits.

Ending the LLC

Under the law of numerous states, unless the operating agreement says otherwise when one member wants to leave the company then the company will dissolve. In this case, the members must fulfill any business obligations that remain, pay off any debts, divide the profits and assets amongst themselves, and then decide where they want to begin a new company to continue the business with the rest of the members.

The operating agreement can prevent this kind of ending to the business by having a buy-sell or buyout provision that's set up with guidelines for what will occur when one member dies, retires, is disabled, or otherwise leaves the company to pursue other interest.

So now you know some of the basics of creating a Limited Liability Company, but why would you want to? Let's explore that in the following chapter.

Chapter 2 - How to Raise Capital to Start an LLC

Is capital an issue when it comes to forming an LLC? Well, while the administrative cost of registering an LLC is minimal, the capital required to begin operations is usually the greatest the company will ever need in lump sum during its existence. If the LLC is entering into distribution, for instance, you need capital to buy trucks; money to put up storage facilities for your merchandise; and even funds to cater for wages and salaries in the initial few months before the business can stand on its own. If the LLC is set to enter the manufacturing sector, there is machinery to acquire; grounds to lease or buy; licenses to pay for; raw materials to purchase; and a host of other things to pay for upfront.

For that reason, investors need to consider the possible sources of capital during the preliminaries of starting an LLC, to ensure success in establishing the LLC and also its sustainability. In fact, every person who decides to establish an LLC needs to have a business plan, and a good one at that, because often, there is need to borrow from external sources; people who need to see how you intend to repay what they lend you.

And do you know how many businesses are striving to get a piece of funding from the limited sources available? Well, records indicate that as at 2009, businesses in the US were in excess of 29 million. And guess what? 98% of them fell under the category of small size businesses, which means that most of them were in dire need of financing. So the better you understand financing and its intricacies, the better for your business.

Here are some options of raising capital:

Own assets

There are many items that fall under this category of personal assets and they include:

- Cash savings

- Personal possessions like jewelry that you can choose to liquidate

- A home against which you can borrow a home equity loan to invest in your business

- Real estate property that you can either sell to raise cash or one that you can use as collateral when borrowing from a bank or such other financing institution

- A retirement fund that you can borrow from with a commitment to repay the borrowed amount within the stipulated short time frame

Before picking on any of the choices available under personal assets, you need to evaluate the risk in each of them. For example, if you borrow against your home and the business fails to pick up, your risk goes beyond losing your business and extends to losing your home. And when you borrow from your retirement fund, any delays in repayment attract hefty penalties, some in form of taxes; not to mention that fees for withdrawing from retirement funds are high.

Informal borrowing

Informal borrowing refers to the monies that you borrow without official procedures – money you borrow from family members or even friends. The reason this ends up being a popular source of initial capital is that as you begin your venture into business, lending institutions do not know you because you are not yet established in the business arena. So you have no business whose strength can be assessed by potential lenders and you have no borrowing history to show your reliability in repaying loans. Yet people in your social circle know you in person and know your integrity.

Of course the fact that it may be easier to raise funds from family and friends does not negate the magnitude of risk that exists in the long run in the event that you fail to repay those funds. You risk losing valuable relationships and you need to think long and hard if you want to put such closeness in jeopardy.

Incorporating other members

If some other people whom you trust accept your invitation to join you in starting your company, it becomes much easier to raise start-up capital. Each one of you has a comparatively smaller amount of money to contribute as opposed to when the LLC was a one-person venture.

Besides, sharing ownership of an LLC means that you can benefit from the professional experience of each one of you without having to pay for consultancy. At the same time, you stand to expand your network of business partners when you are more than one investor. In fact, you can also not understate the importance of the network of friends that each person brings on board. This is because you enter into business with the intention of making sales and the more friends you have the more likely you are to expand your sales network, increase your sales and have sustainable sales levels.

Use of credit cards

You need to look at credit cards as convenient sources of funds, but which are only great for short-term financing. They are convenient because you can use your personal card and receive your money in an instance, as opposed to bank loans that can take long time to process. Even administratively, the process of securing a bank loan is comparatively complex because you need to have a good business plan in place in addition to other bits of evaluation.

Of course credit cards have their motivation, including offers that come in form of travel awards; sometimes absence of annual fee; cash back on the basis of size of purchases; and so on. So you can count on a credit card to meet your immediate financial needs in establishing your LLC. All you need to do is put it high on the list of priorities when it comes to settling of debts.

Conventional lenders

Even as a new entrant to the business world, you still can try to secure financing from conventional lenders such as banks, credit unions and such other financing institutions. However, you will need to wait longer than if you were getting funds from other sources because the protocol in these institutions is a bit complex. You cannot, for instance, by pass the investors' business plan and often the lender will demand collateral. In other cases, the lender may even require that you bring along a guarantor who is already known to the bank or in the business arena.

As a new entrant in the business arena, do not be discouraged if the conventional lenders turn you down. Do not take it personally as it is in their tradition to cover all the loopholes that could spell risk in loan repayment.

Special loan programs

Sometimes the federal government and even the state authorities set aside certain monies to be advanced to investors in clearly defined categories. So as you do due diligence before starting your company, you need to look into the possibility of sourcing financing from such special funds.

Examples of such fund categories:

- Grants to military veterans

- Loans from micro-finance lenders

- Funds meant for specific regions, some based on economic marginalization

- Funds meant as incentives in certain industries such as investment in production and distribution of alternative energy

- Funds availed by non-governmental organizations (NGOs) for specific reasons

Online lending sites

Today it is possible to borrow money from individual or institutions without having to meet in person. Mostly, such lending takes place through what is referred to commonly as Peer to Peer (P2P) lending sites. The lenders' decision whether to lend you money or not and to what proportions depends on your creditworthiness as far as the lenders can ascertain. Good examples of such lending sites include the *Lending Club* as well as *Prosper*.

Consolidating funds for starting off business is the hardest part. Thereafter, there are more individuals and institutions willing to advance your company cash because you have tangible assets to use as collateral, Local Purchase Orders to show as guarantee for future sales; some history with the bank; and so on. In short, securing financing for your daily operations is not as difficult as securing funds to start off the business.

Common sources of working capital for LLCs include merchant cash advancing institutions, institutions that help through receivable factoring, and others that support you through equipment financing, etc.

To B (Borrow) Or Not to B?

When it comes to financing businesses, there are 2 parties: investors and lenders. Both of them can provide you with the necessary funds or capitalization for putting up or expanding your business and each of them have their own pros and cons. As such, which is better for your planned LLC?

To help you determine which is which, let's take a look at both debt (borrowed money) and equity (your or other people's capital investment).

Debt

When you finance your LLC with debt, it means you will borrow money from others with the obligation of paying back the amount you borrowed – along with a pre-agreed upon interest rate – at a specified payment date in the future.

One good example of debt is secured loans, such as those given by banks and other lending institutions. Secured loans are – as the name suggests – secured with collateral that the financial institution can foreclose to settle your debt in case you aren't able to pay it as agreed upon. Typically, secured loans are gradually paid back with monthly installments, which require the personal guarantee of the borrower. Some of the resources or assets that you can use as collateral for borrowing money from banks for the purpose of putting up or expanding your LLC are real estate, insurance policies, equipment, accounts receivables and inventory. In case you're not able to pay back the loan, the lending financial institution will take possession of your collateral in settlement of your financial obligation.

In the United States, the US Small Business Administration or US-SBA can act as guarantor for different types of loans for small businesses. Given that SBA-guaranteed bank loans have much lower risks for the lending banks compared to those that are guaranteed merely by the business owner, taking out such loans are significantly less costly. Normally, SBA-guaranteed loans have lower interest rates and longer terms due to its low credit risk (for the bank). Business owners of loans approved for SBA guarantee also don't need to put up much by way of collateral compared to when getting a loan from the same banks without such guarantee.

SBA loans, however, aren't for everybody who wants to start a small business and get funding. Because the government is guaranteeing the loan and it's using public funds to do so, they need to exercise a greater deal of responsibility by being more stringent in screening applicants for such guarantees. If you have a very poor credit score or history, you may want to consider other sources of financing because those will be considered in the very stringent credit evaluation process of the US-SBA.

Other alternative sources of debt financing may include factoring, loans from family and friends, merchant advances and credit cards (personal or business). Some of these alternative sources, like merchant advances, are paid back as a percentage of your monthly or weekly sales instead of a monthly fixed payment. Of course, these have their own disadvantages, particularly higher interest rates and shorter terms.

While some entrepreneurs stay away from debt financing like it's a plague or something, borrowing money can be advantageous in some ways, the first being is that it can fund businesses of practically any size.

According to John Fleming, the SBA Delaware office's district director, the SBA offers different lending programs that give all kinds of entrepreneur's access to much needed capital. According to him, they offer small business loans on the least end of the spectrum and on the huge end, multi-million dollar commercial loans that can be paid in as long as 20 years at a fixed interest rate.

And while SBA-guaranteed loans offer entrepreneurs much by way of benefits especially in terms of funding small business ventures, there are many other options than just regular loans from banking institutions. And this wide array of financing options is a key advantage debt financing has over funding through equity.

Alternative lenders tend to charge higher interest rates simply because they take on more credit risk, i.e., the possibility that the amount they lend won't be paid back whether in part or in full. The reason they're referred to as "alternative" is because they're the creditors of second and third – or even last – resort for borrowers who weren't able to pass the relatively stringent qualifications of traditional lenders like banks. In particular, they have less than ideal credit scores or insufficient collateral.

Another benefit of using debt is higher return on capital or equity (ROE), which is computed by dividing net income over equity. Because interest paid on debt is tax deductible, it reduces your tax expense. But you may say it will also reduce your profitability. In terms of absolute amount, yes but in terms of ROE, no. Consider this example:

	No Debt	50% Debt
Assets	$200,000.00	$200,000.00
Debt	$0.00	$100,000.00
Equity	$200,000.00	$100,000.00
Gross Sales	$100,000.00	$100,000.00
Less: Operating Expenses	$80,000.00	$80,000.00
Gross Income	$20,000.00	$20,000.00
Less: Interest Expense	$0.00	$5,000.00
Net Income	$20,000.00	$15,000.00
Equity	$200,000.00	$100,000.00
Return On Equity	10.00%	15.00%

As you can see, by funding 50% of the business' assets with debt, you can actually make your money more productive. By using debt financing, you can invest the other $100,000 in equally if not more profitable ventures.

The last benefit of funding your LLC using debt is control. With debt, your creditors don't have a say in terms of how you run your LLC. Equity or capital investors on the other hand have such say because they're part owners with you. As soon as you pay back your loan, your relationship with the creditor is over but with investors, the relationship continues until the LLC is dissolved or until they divest their interests in the LLC either to you or someone else.

But as with all things, debt also has its downside. For one, if your LLC is cash-strapped to begin with, you'll be spending a good chunk of your revenues on repaying the loan. The single biggest challenge or disadvantage in financing your LLC with debt is also the most obvious – repayment. As such, some finance experts believe that using debt is also counter profitable.

Another disadvantage to financing your LLC with debt is the regular fixed payments, which is particularly true for most debt financing schemes. In most cases, periodic payments are done monthly and this is regardless of how well – or bad – your LLC is actually doing in terms of profitability. This means your LLC is at risk of being unable to miss a payment – or more – if revenues dip significantly for certain periods of time. And missed payments may result in charges and added interest expenses that can further exacerbate an already challenged financial performance.

Equity

When we talk about equity financing, especially in the small businesses sector, it refers to financing through capital, which is either your or other people's money. When using other people's money for equity financing, you give the equity investors part ownership of the company so instead of just having a claim to a portion of your LLC's resources, as in the case of debt financing, they have a claim to a proportionate ownership of all the LLC's resources, including its profits. That's why I mentioned earlier that one of the advantages of debt is control, i.e., creditors aren't part owners and as such, don't have a say in the way you'll run the LLC. Equity investors are part owners and as such, have a say in the way the LLC will be run.

For most small businesses, family and friends are the usual sources of equity financing. Investments of family and friends are normally paid back to them via buyback of their shares in the business as soon as the business starts making money, which may happen within several years. As a compromise, most small business owners link the buyback of initial investors' shares in the business to the operating cash flows. That way, the investors don't need to wait forever to get their money back – should they want to – and the business owner's cash flows aren't strained.

Family and friends are the normal sources of equity financing for start up businesses because at that point, entrepreneurs still don't have the ability to source capital from traditional financing sources, whether it's equity or debt. And as soon as a start up starts making money and establishing itself as a solid business, it can attract investors or venture capitalists.

While venture capitalists and "angel" investors are often lumped into one, they are actually different. Angel investors are "people" while venture capitalists are normally companies or firms. Angel investors' investments range from just $25 to $100 grand while venture capitalist firms' investments can go as high as $7 million or higher.

While equity financing isn't a one-size-fits-all-entrepreneurs kind of financing, it has its own benefits that may make it worth the while. And two of these happen to be the two biggest gripes against debt financing: cash flow and personal liability. As mentioned earlier, equity financing doesn't require regular payments to the investors and as such, it doesn't draw capital away from the enterprise. And if you're able to get others to provide equity financing for your LLC, you get to share the business' risks with them too.

If you use equity financing to fund your LLC, you also don't need to pay your investors back – well, at least right away. This means your LLC can take its time to grow before buying back the investors' shares in the business, should they choose to get their money back eventually. If they're in it for the long haul, you don't even have to make payments on their investments other than their shares in the LLCs profits.

Lastly, given that equity investors are part owners of the LLC, there's no obligation to pay them back should the LLC fold and close shop, unlike with creditors.

Equity financing can be disadvantageous if equity investors' share in the LLC can be enough to wrestle control away from you. As mentioned earlier, equity investors are your co-owners and as such, they earned the right to have much say in the LLC. Equity partners can influence the operations and culture of a company in both positive and negative ways. As such, most – if not all – entrepreneurs prefer to maintain control over their businesses. Having a financial partner getting in the way of them running their business in the manner they deem most fit is the last they want.

The best way to prevent this is to limit equity investments of others to 49% at the most. That way, you still retain a minimum ownership of 51%, which is enough to give you majority control over the LLC. Giving other equity investors the opportunity to gain control can cause you significant problems, especially if you want to fund future capital expenditures or operations with debt, which is what many entrepreneurs do. It's because most equity investors won't sign up for additional debt financing and if by any chance they own a significant portion of the LLC, it'll be very challenging for you to source additional funding.

Small to medium-sized entrepreneurs (I'm referring to their businesses, not their personal sizes) also don't have much say or control as to when equity investors will get out of the business. Typically, private equity investors want to get out of start-ups within 5 to 7 years and by that time, they usually gain significant control to make it happen. Often times, business owners don't like it.

Debt or Equity?

Ultimately, the choice between debt or equity financing – or the optimal mix of such – will depend on what's more important to you and your LLC.

Chapter 3 – Benefits

Limited Liability Companies are one of the most flexible options for a business entity. They allow the creator to choose how to distribute profits, decide who will manage the affairs of the business, and decide how the profits will be taxed, which we'll discuss in a later chapter. They also offer a ton in terms of liability protection.

Once you decide to enter into business, you need to weigh the available options and choose the one that suits you best. If, for instance, you are not exactly clear how big you want your business to be or how wide you want your scope to be, an LLC may be your best bet. Not only is it flexible in the kind of businesses it can accommodate, but it has more benefits than a sole proprietorship, a partnership or even a corporate entity.

Here are the main benefits:

Personal Liability Protection:

Creditors who would like their money or lawsuits that have

been filed against the business will not affect the owner personally unless the business owner wishes it to. The business owner can make it so that no matter what, their family's possessions are in safe keeping.

Business Liability Protection:

Limited Liability Companies are one of the only company forms that are able to prevent a personal lawsuit and creditors from liquidating the business in order to fulfill a judgment.

No Ownership Restrictions:

Other entities are able to be owners and as many people who want to be owners of the company can be. There are no limits.

No Management Restrictions:

Owners are able to manage and managers are able to own the company. It's all up to the people who are making the company.

Flexible Tax Status:

There are many different ways a limited liability company can be taxed. The owner can choose the best form for their company as they're starting it.

No Separate Tax Returns:

With a regular limited liability company, the business's losses and profits will be reported on the owner's tax returns. If there's more than one owner, they have to use the percentage of gains or losses the business allows them.

No Double Taxation:

Unlike other structures of business, limited liability companies are able to have a pass-through taxation. That means the profits will not be taxed at the company level, only at the individual level.

Flexible Profit Distribution:

The company owner is able to decide what percentage of the profit will be given to whom, no matter how much of the company that person actually owns.

Easy to customize

If your intention is to run a small size business and you register an LLC, nothing about the LLC will hinder your operations. Neither the state law nor the reality of operation restricts you from running a small size business as an LLC. And when you decide you want to expand your business capacity and run your business as medium size, you can proceed without any formalities. In fact, there is so much flexibility operating as an LLC that it accommodates a 2-person business as well as it accommodates a business with tens of investors. In short, the size of the business does not complicate the way you write your operating agreement. After all, an LLC allows you to draft the rules that suit your type of business as well as the relationship you have with one another as business owners.

You cannot get this kind of flexibility with a corporation. There are far too many formalities with the way you run a corporation, and you have to rigidly follow the laid down procedures. Even the official infrastructure provided by the state where shareholders and directors as well as corporate officers fit is quite rigid.

Easy to protect business real estate assets

When your big assets are in the name of your LLC, nobody can go suing you and attempting to attach your assets on flimsy grounds. The LLC is a stronger entity than an individual, capable of hiring a reputable attorney; and so not many people will attempt to push it around. So simply by operating as an LLC, you can avoid probate for the most part and keep your estate protected.

Convenient in shielding intellectual property

Sometimes you have more than one intellectual property, possibly because you are dealing with different products or even different LLCs. Ordinarily each LLC protects its own property rights but when you have a number of LLCs it may be a bit of a hassle and even kind of clumsy. So you may be better off having one operating company handling all your intellectual properties so that any trademarks that you have, your patents or even copyrights are handled and protected by that one LLC. And by protecting we mean officially registering them and doing all the necessary administrative and legal paperwork so that it is clear to all and sundry that those are legitimately your intellectual properties.

Easier to raise initial capital

One of the most difficult things to do when you really want to initiate a business is raising enough capital to start off; what you may call seed capital. It is even more difficult because not many sources can lend you long-term when you are a novice, or more appropriately running a start-up business. And often, the close friends or relatives who may be willing to lend you cannot provide enough to meet your fixed costs and initial operating costs.

However, when it comes to LLCs, there are financial institutions that are prepared to lend start-up capital to small and medium size businesses. At the same time, just by the sheer fact that there is usually more than one person formally bound in business and with serious shareholding stakes, an LLC attracts funding from lending institutions more readily than either a sole proprietorship or a partnership. It just reflects stability and hence better credibility and reliability as far as ability to service loans is concerned. And of course, it is normally easier to raise sizeable capital from a number of people than just one or two partners.

Convenient for project of a short term nature

Did you know that in the beginning when LLCs were entered into the statutes it was envisaged that investors would use them for short term project? And that is why there is a place for you to indicate the date you intend to dissolve the LLC right in the articles of incorporation. In short, it is expected that you can tell roughly for how long your project is going to last. So right from the inception, LLCs were meant to suit short term projects pretty well. LLCs were not seen as structures suited to last perpetually and indefinitely like corporations.

Actually, the projects that were thought ideal for LLCs included film related projects, real estate development and such others. Today, however, much as LLCs are still great for short term projects, they are also good for long term projects; even those that are meant to last indefinitely.

Good option for segregation of assets

The fact that you can hold some assets in your personal capacity and others as a member of an LLC or even the real owner of it means that you don't hold all your eggs in the same basket. Obviously, it means that if things go wrong on the business front you still have your personal assets intact; and if anything jeopardizes your personal assets then you have a buffer in your LLC.

Flexibility in distribution of profits

In an LLC, you do not have to adhere strictly maintain the

profit distribution ratios that you started with. You can make adjustments as and when you wish based on mutually agreed basis. Sometimes it could be purely in the interest of motivation to investors.

Flexibility of location

An LLC is one form of entity that you can run from whatever location you choose to. If you think a certain state favors you because of its tax regime, you can go ahead and form your LLC there. The only thing you cannot afford to do is form your LLC in one state and go ahead to carry on your business in another state for the sake of evading tax.

The reason for that warning is that if you try to evade any business tax in a state that is facilitating your operations, you are going to get caught sooner or later; and the consequences are not pleasant. You must realize that the activity in your business bank account is an easy give-away just as are business cards, credit card bills and such other documents. So, choose your location as you wish as long as you don't try to cheat the IRS.

Still, there are some businesses that provide even more flexibility of location. If, for instance, you are carrying out your business online, there is no reason why you cannot register in a state of your choice. After all, there are no transactions that will require you to knock onto a physical office door in any state. And you cannot be accused of enjoying physical infrastructure in one state but paying taxes in another. So in that sense, LLCs whose business is web based accords you more flexibility as far as official business location is concerned.

Flexibility of composition

It is easier to add new members in your LLC than it is to add them in a partnership or a corporation. Individuals can also easily sell their interest in the LLC in a more convenient manner. When you want to sell your interest, you don't need the consent of your business partners or formal meetings of the Board of Directors with minutes being taken for that purpose. In short, LLC have minimal administrative hurdles and relatively few restrictions.

Easy registration procedure

Apart from sole proprietorship, an LLC may be the next easiest business entity to formally register. It has an easy structure and calls for minimal documentation. In fact, you can handle the formation process all on your own without having to engage an attorney. And once you have accomplished that all you need is obtain an Employer ID Number (EIN) from the offices of the IRS and then open your business bank account and you are good to go.

And even if you want to engage an attorney, the fee is very reasonable. In the state of Oregon, for instance, the fee for filing for registration has for sometime been just $100.

Now that you know some of the benefits of forming a limited liability company let's move on to the ten things you'll want avoid as you begin your company.

Chapter 4 - 10 Things to Avoid

Limited liability companies are very powerful setups where the company owner is able to do some pretty amazing things. However, there is the old saying that with great power there is great responsibility. Otherwise, if you don't watch out, you'll get yourself into a lot of trouble. This chapter is about helping you avoid hot water.

Here are the top ten mistakes limited liability company owners make.

#1 Fraudulent Transference of Assets

If you were recently sued and wanted to protect your assets, then it's already too late. If you transferred your assets into the limited liability company, you'd be fraudulently conveying those assets. According to the law, you're fraudulently conveying assets when you do one of the two following things:

- You sell or transfer the assets at less than a fair-market value, which will result in the creditor being defrauded.

- You transfer the assets so that the creditor is not able to seize those assets or recoup the claim.

A fraudulent conveyance is a civil offense and has the ability to cost you a lot more money in the long run than if you were just to hand over the possessions in question. If you formed a limited liability company with the intent to defraud a creditor rather than forming a limited liability company not knowing that the assets were immediately at risk, you're pretty bad off. Not only will the creditor be able to get the assets, but in some states, you'll be subject to penalties that might include prison time. In addition, federal laws say that if you knowingly commit fraudulent conveyance, then it's a criminal offense.

It's possible to mistakenly and illegally convey assets. This occurs when you're planning the asset security plan and moving assets into the limited liability company or two and a lawsuit is already pending against you that you don't know about yet. Even though you're not aware of the pending lawsuit, the assets have still been fraudulently conveyed. You most likely won't have criminal charges brought against you at this point, but you still might be required to turn over the assets you thought were protected.

#2 Evading Taxes

While it's prudent for the company owner to take every action the law allows for them to reduce their tax burden, evading taxes is definitely against the law. Tax evasion is when the owner of a company or the company itself dodges paying taxes through illegal ways. Tax avoidance, on the other hand, is acceptable and legal. This just means that the company legally reduces the amount of tax it owes. For example, putting a retirement savings in a Roth IRA that allows you to defer taxes is considered tax avoidance. It's perfectly legal to reduce your tax burden this way.

To figure out whether you're avoiding or evading taxes, remember this: tax avoidance happens when you avoid the creation of tax liability to begin with. However, you or the company is guilty of tax evasion when something has been done to owe taxes, but they're not paid. Then the owner of the company will most likely end up in prison.

The scariest thing about tax evasion is that it's a felony, which doesn't have any regard for how much tax you evaded. Just five hundred dollars evaded in taxes is the same as five million dollars in the eyes of the law.

#3 Choosing a Bad Partner

The partnership within your company should be like a marriage. You have to jump into it with your eyes completely open. Fifty percent of marriages in the United States end in divorce, and the numbers are actually a lot worse for business partnerships. This shouldn't be a deterrent to you because when you have a partner that you work well with, the efforts will be rewarded greatly. You have to make sure that:

- You know the person you're going into business with.

- You have the procedures and policies to go by when disagreements come up, and they are going to happen!

When you're first starting your business, you'll be sitting down with your partner and agreeing on where the both of you want the company to go and what you want your percentage of ownership and roles in the company to be. The problems usually come about years after the company has been started, when one of the partner's lives goes in different directions. For example, you might want to expand into a new market but your partner is happy with their income and doesn't want to expand the business. They want to let it keep coasting. Or your partner wants cash and they want to sell out, but you don't have the cash lying around to purchase their share. In these moments, there needs to be a plan.

There has to be an operating agreement or partnership agreement. Sit down with all of the partners in the business and plan the partnership all the way to the end.

#4 Ignoring Bureaucratic Paperwork

Tax returns, state filings, permits, and so on and so forth are all time consuming, bureaucratic, and you most likely would rather stick your thumb in your eye than do them. You're not alone in this sentiment. However, it's extremely important that you don't drop the ball and stay on top of all that paperwork.

This especially goes for state filings. The limited liability company is registered under the laws of the state, and they can easily take away your right to operate. If you don't keep up with the filings, the state will revoke the limited liability company license, and you'll most likely be operating as if you were a sole proprietorship without your knowledge. There will be zero liability protection if the company is taken to court.

#5 *Trademark Infringement*

Encroaching on another company's trademark is one of the easiest mistakes in business and can end up costing your business and you a fortune. Be cautious about infringing on someone else's trademark because not only are you able to fall into this trap without knowing it, but many Fortune 500 companies hold hundreds of trademarks. They have paralegals and attorneys who spend their entire day scouring the local communities and internet for small businesses that could be infringing on their trademark. Companies are then nice enough to send the small company a cease and desist letter.

If you receive one of these letters, you have two options.

First, if you're an upstart and you don't have a ton of money wrapped up in the name that the company is disputing, stop using that name and choose another one.

If you spent a ton of time and money marketing with that name and feel that you have the right to use it and that it doesn't confuse the consumers, you could consider hiring a good attorney. The trademark attorney will point you in the proper direction, then. Just keep in mind that if you end up in court, you'll be spending a lot of money, especially if the opponent is someone who has a lot of money.

#6 Not Making an Operating Agreement

Some parts of putting up a business are fun such as designing a logo, thinking of a name for the business, refining the offered product, and planning its future expansion, among others. And then there are the really boring parts like crafting an operating agreement.

What is an operating agreement? Also referred to as partnership agreement in the case of multi-member LLCs, it's a legal document where each person's responsibilities and rights and the way the company will be run – including day-to-day operations, LLC dissolution or a member's death – are clearly defined.

While operating agreements are not legally required to begin a limited liability company, you'd be remiss if you did not make one. Limited liability companies can make up a lot of their own rules. All you have to do is put them into the operating agreement. If an operating agreement does not exist, then the state laws will automatically apply through default. Allowing the state government to tell you how to run and structure your business is probably not the best idea. You not only miss one of the major benefits of a limited liability company, flexibility, but you are also not in control of your business.

However, boring it may be, it's one of the most important things you'll need to accomplish even before putting in the money and time into your LLC. In fact, some states legally mandate that you create your LLCs partnership or operating agreement.

Hiring a lawyer isn't needed to come up with an operating agreement. You can check out the websites of your local bar organizations for starting point samples. The New York State bar, for example, posted such samples and SCORE provides workshops, templates and articles to help new entrepreneurs.

Once you've gotten your draft done, I highly recommend that you hire a solo-practicing lawyer to go through your draft just to make sure everything's in order. Solo-practitioners normally charge lower compared to big-firm lawyers and as such, it'll also come out cheaper for you.

Make a real operating agreement that is unique to the company and then use that agreement. You should read over this agreement occasionally to refresh your memory about your company's policies when it comes to certain issues. If you decide to change the policy, that's okay, too. Just make sure that there is a meeting with the other members of the agreement who can vote on the changes. Meeting procedures should be found in your operating agreement.

There are many clauses you can include in your operating agreement but of them all, ensure that these are included:

- Capital Contributions: In this clause, the amount of money each member needs to put in for starting up the LLC is clearly defined. It should also say what the next action steps are in case more money is needed to keep the LLC going and become profitable such as closing shop, getting outside investors, or borrowing money, among others.

- Making Decisions: In this clause, you and your partners must clearly identify how decisions regarding the LLC's operations are to be made by whom and at what levels. Do you need a quorum, a majority vote or a unanimous decision to move ahead?

- Dissolution: This is probably the Clause that no one wants to talk about. However morbid it may sound, this clause is crucial and must be discussed at the start of any business relationship, whether it's a partnership, LLC or a corporation. As early as at the beginning, it is important to figure out what will happen in the event of the LLC being dissolved for one reason or another. Since the LLC is just being started, everyone is still getting along well, which makes it easier to discuss the prospects of an eventual dissolution. Consider the fact that it can be much, much harder to discuss dissolution and exit strategies towards the end of your LLC's life when things may already be quite stressful.

- Death or Disability: However unlikely, really bad things can happen to you and the other members of the LLC. As such, better be prepared than be caught off guard. In this clause, wills, trusts and insurance policies will be tackled. Given that, you really have to think well about who you would like to entrust the LLC's decision making responsibilities on your behalf, who will takeover your stake in the LLC and whether or not your beneficiaries will have a say in the LLC in the event that you pass away.

- Distributions or Salaries: Technically speaking these are different clauses but still, they're hinting at basically the same thing. When tackling or coming up with this clause, you can begin by asking basic questions such as when can the partners take their money out of the business in case they'd like to, will the LLC's members be repaid for their Investments and if so, when will that happen, among other questions on salaries, profit sharing and getting back investments.

#7 Not Documenting Company Activities

Limited liability law is pretty relaxed when it comes to keeping records, but don't allow that to fool you. Documenting the company's activities is still very important. At some point, the business decisions will most likely be questioned, and there will be relief when you have your company documents there to defend your choices. Not only this, but the company records will prove that you've done everything by the book. Therefore, if an angry member sues because they didn't get their way at the last meeting, then you can demonstrate that the correct vote was performed and that the right procedures were taken.

Here are a few good reasons to keep a company's records straight:

- When applying for a loan or creating a bank relationship, the record keeping will elude that you're a good business owner.

- The most common lawsuit between members of a limited liability company occurs when one or more members disagree with a course of action that another member took. By properly documenting actions, the owner is able to prove they went through the right channels and acted on decisions according to their powers described in the operating agreement.

- If you ever want to take the company public, sell it, or enter into a joint venture, then you'll need the previous company's actions properly recorded.

- If the IRS ever audits you, they will want to see a record of the company's transactions and their resulting actions to see the intentions behind the transactions.

#8 Treating the Company like A Personal Bank

This is actually rather simple and important. Only use the company's money for company-related expenses. It sounds elementary, but it's a common mistake that will cost you a ton in the long-run, not only in penalties to the IRS, but it will also cost you the liability protection you have. It's often tempting to write a check or use a debit card from whatever account has the most money in it, but don't do it. Personal expenses that you'll want to avoid are things like groceries and a mortgage or personal debt. Restaurant bills are all right, as long as the dining experience was business-related, like a job interview or meeting.

If you really want to pay for a personal item out of the company's bank account, then do it. Just make sure this doesn't happen often and that you properly document this transaction as a loan or officer income. If the transaction was large, then you'll want to document it in the company minutes, too.

#9 Neglecting to Foreign File

Performing interstate business has become a lot easier as the world has become a lot smaller. Every state has a different idea of what transacting business really means. Regardless, you're required to register to transact business in every state that you operate in.

Here are some questions you should ask yourself to figure out if you're transacting business in a specific state:

- Does the company have a physical location in the state, like a corporate office or manufacturing facility?

- Do you accept orders in or originating from the state?

- Do you have employees in that state?

- Do you have a bank account in that state?

#10 Refusing to Delegate

Some people will trust no one to help them and will want to do everything themselves. This is because they believe no one else can handle the job as well as they're able to. This is a disease of the self-employed people out there, and it can weaken them a lot. Why? Because they can only do so much and until they begin to delegate, the organization is never going to grow. Not to mention that they'll most likely get burned out before they know it.

Knowing when to delegate some things in business will enable you to avoid getting into trouble. For example, tax laws are very complex and unless the owner has studied to be an accountant, there's a good chance that if the owner handles the taxes, what they don't know will destroy them, especially if the business has employees, is large, and is complex.

The same goes for legal advice from attorneys. Company owners should never try to represent themselves in court. Lawyers, while they might be expensive, are very necessary to a small business. Don't operate on assumptions. The company owner should seek the knowledge of a good lawyer when legal matters are in question.

When handling corporate filings, especially if the business is registered in more than one state, a registered agent should assist the owner. Not only is the registered agent required by law, but they have more knowledge and resources in a corporate matter than an owner does. Use a registered agent whose part of a competent company. That way, the owner and company can save money when seeking information about non-complex, simple corporate matters or getting answers about the filings.

Don't be a jack of all trades! The company owner should master just one thing and delegate the rest to employees or outside firms. For example, if the owner is not that great at sales, then hire a sales manager and empower that person to take the reins and build a great sales floor. Even if the company owner is decent at something, find someone who is better and recruit him or her. When you find them, take a leap of faith and don't undermine them. After all, the business is only as good as the people who are in it.

Now that you know the top ten mistakes a limited liability company makes and how to avoid them let's talk about how to give the company a great name.

Chapter 5 - Giving Your Limited Liability Company a Great Name

You can't just expect a great name to fall out of thin air for your company. Creativity is best when the person who needs it is using a few helpful restrictions. The following are a few naming rules for a business.

- **Be Distinct:** Naming a brand-new and improved social media site MyTube or FaceSpace is not going to give the impression that the company is new or improved. It's going to have the opposite effect, actually.

- **Be Memorable:** Avoid any acronyms, and unless you have a huge annual marketing budget you can waste. If you really feel the need to shorten the length of your company name, then condense it into an amalgam such as Nabisco, which stands for National Biscuit Company. With that said, differing to what you might hear somewhere else, long names are actually more notable than a short name. Think of TGIFriday's and Joe's. So don't burden yourself over restricting yourself when it comes to length, especially because you'll have improved luck finding an online domain name with a longer name rather than a shorter one.

- **Be Welcoming:** By this, I mean that you should make sure the name is easy to pronounce. No one wants to avoid saying the name because they're afraid they'll mispronounce it. Try out potential names on a young child. If they can't pronounce it, get rid of hit and have them help you find an alternative. Kids are pretty good when it comes to ideas!

- **Be Meaningful:** This doesn't really mean that you have to be descriptive. You want to save the descriptiveness for taglines and slogans. Make the name evocative and allude to the soul of the business. For example, Netflix is a really good name for online video rental sites, but FilmsOnline is not.

- **Be Vivid:** What image and feeling do you want the customer to associate with the brand of the business? Try to paint a picture for them. For example, the name Stonyfield Farm makes you think of a few longhorns in a pasture that was an old farm field. This gives the impression of wholesomeness.

- **Be Bold:** Because so many names are already taken out there, you can't be scared to take a risk. As long as the name is evocative, then don't worry about being unusual. Just look at Google and Yahoo!

- **Be Eternal:** Limited liability companies are now made in order to have a continuous life, so why limit the existence of the business with the name? Choose a name that will sound great for centuries down the road, or you could face some conundrums like Twentieth Century Fox did.

- **Be Expansive:** You don't want the name of the company to restrict your business to a certain location, service, or product. For example, Los Angeles Rentals would need to spend a lot of money on rebranding their company if they were going to go into another marketplace. No matter how small the company is now, don't allow your name keep you from succeeding as the business moves onward.

- **Be Global:** Be sure the company name is internationally friendly. Otherwise, you might be ready to expand abroad in the future and you'll one day find out that your name has a negative meaning in another culture.

Domain Names

With the proliferation of the internet, it is also important to think of a good domain name for your LLC, in case you'd like to put up a website for it. It is also becoming more challenging to find simple domain names, especially those made up of just one English word. As such, coming up with a memorable and search friendly domain name is an important name-generating activity for your LLC.

Because there are so many web pages on the Internet right now, it's best to go for a domain name that is spelled as close as possible to how it's pronounced or sounds. If you don't, not only when you still have to spell out your LLC's name to others, it may also be harder for people to discover your LLC's page online. Two examples of companies that did not adhere to this wise advice are Flickr and Digg.

And speaking of search friendly and memorable names for your LLC's domain, here are some very helpful tips to help you come up with a great domain name for your LLC:

- Ditch the short names: If you're thinking you can still find a domain name that's less then six letters, think again. The bad news is most, if not all, of them are already taken either by squatters or legitimate businesses.

- Phrase Play: Playing around with words can help you come up with a great domain name for your LLC. A good example is a website called lightmyfire.com, which is from a company that manufactures candles.

- Think Out of the Country: Other businesses use a foreign word as their domain name. Consider the computer brand Acer, which means sharp or acute in Latin, or Ubuntu, which is taken from the African system of philosophy on interpersonal relations and allegiances. They're easy to remember because of their unique sound, brevity and closeness to being spelled as they are pronounced.

- Don't Put Too Much Premium On Trendiness: While optimizing your domain name for keywords searches may sound like a good idea, it is only for the short term considering that search engines continually tweak their algorithms, which can render your domain name's ability to rank high in current search engine results obsolete after a while. Better to create landing pages that are keyword search friendly, which you'll then use to direct visitors to your LLC's main page.

- Dot-Com Supremacy: While a lot of people believe that any domain name that doesn't end with a ".com" is inferior, it's hogwash. What determines whether or not your LLC's domain name is memorable, catchy and searchable is not the prefix but the actual name. So don't worry if "dot-com" domain names are no longer available for your desired name.

Brand Name

Occasionally, businesses change their names as part of their rebranding activities. This is brought about by business mistakes or simply by mistakenly choosing a forgettable weak business name. And because prevention is better than cure, it's best that as you brand your LLC from the get go, you take the time and effort to come up with a good one. Don't rush your brand name.

A common mistake normally committed by many new entrepreneurs is choosing a brand name that reflects their names. Do your LLC a favor by not doing the same. While it can feel good to have your business named or branded after yourself, there are good reasons to stay clear from an eponymous (named after a person – you) brand or business name.

It'll be easier to promote your LLC to investors and customers if its future isn't connected to yours. Naming your

LLC after yourself will give the impression that it is a single-person operation. Plus, naming your LLC or brand after yourself won't do a good job of telling the story, profile or character of your LLC. Why? Because your name is only relevant to a few people.

Another reason to avoid being narcissistic about your LLC's name is the possibility of your LLC expanding to other profitable lines. For example, if you're into the business of selling bikes, don't pigeonhole your LLC's name with one that speaks only about mountain bikes. Instead of using a name like Power Trails, a better one would be Pedal Power, which can be applicable to all other bikes as well. Unless you've decided that it's the only market segment your LLC will serve for the rest of its life.

Many starting entrepreneurs are tempted to grab market share and establish themselves as players in the industry they entered as quickly as possible by going for business names that are too functionally and descriptively specific, which end up boxing them to such a small niche. Consider companies like CompUSA and RadioShack, who have been outlasted by a company like Best Buy, whose name doesn't pigeonhole the company to a single type of product or class of products unlike the 2 other companies.

To Trademark or Not to Trademark?

Filing for your business name's trademark isn't necessary in England, Canada and the United States because in those jurisdictions, operating under a particular business name automatically affords you the necessary trademark rights to it. If that's the case, why the state and federal restrictions on trademark in the US?

What it boils down to is your LLC's future. If you don't file for trademark, your LLC's right to its name is only valid within the geographical scope of operations for a given period of time. So if you have plans of going national at some point, you can definitely save your LLC a whole lot of hassle and inconvenience later on by investing a couple of thousands of dollars in a Federal trademark.

However, a trademark by any other name doesn't smell as sweet because not all trademarks are equally strong. In terms of strength, trademarks fall into 5 different categories and your LLC name's category will determine just how much protection it has versus pirates and infringers:

- Arbitrary or Fanciful: These refer to trademarks that had no particular meaning before being utilized as such. In terms of strength, this is the strongest or easiest to defend simply because it only refers to the brand, services or products that bear it. Good examples of these are Polaroid, Verizon and Google.

- Arbitrary: These refer to English words that are considered to be common and are employed in contexts where their usual or real meanings are not related whatsoever to the brand, services or goods to which they're being applied. A very good example of this would be Apple. As a fruit, it's a trademark that can't be defended or protected. But if the word is used in association with electronic products, it is very strong and protectable as a trademark because let's face it, apples have absolutely nothing to do with electronic products, making it a very unique trademark.

- Suggestive: Indirectly, they refer to brands, services or goods that such trademarks are associated. They also need some stretch of imagination for consumers to understand. The trademark is strengthened in people's minds via the secondary or reference meaning. Good examples of this would be Fruit of the Loom, which suggest cloth that's nice and soft and Monster, that suggest inhuman levels of energy.

- Descriptive: Such kinds of trademarks describe the brand, services or goods that they're linked to, marketing wise. This type of trademark is inherently weak or hard to defend but if you can show the regulatory authorities that consumers can only associate your descriptive trademark to your business, you can register that trademark. Good examples of these are Aspirin, Blu-Ray and Quick Print.

- Generic: This type of trademark is the weakest and as such, can't be protected. Why? Because they're too generic, making it virtually impossible to distinguish from others. An example of a generic trademark is a bottled water brand named "water" or a clothing line named "clothes". If you even dare try to file for a trademark for such names, expect the judge to give you the boot quickly.

In case you'll need to go to court to defend your trademark, all jurisdictions subject your trademark to a multiple parts test to evaluate if the trademarks in question can confuse consumers. Visual, meaning and sound similarities of the trademarks concerned comprise the aspects of the first part of the test. The second part takes into consideration the contested services or goods' similarities.

Many entrepreneurs make the mistake of naming their businesses without the benefit of doing any significant research or study to determine if there's already an existing trademark on such. Typically, a secured trademark can be held for anywhere between 5 to 10 years prior to renewal.

Legal Actions

Nothing else can feel like being sucker-punched in the gut than discovering that another business has been operating with a trademark that's very similar to your LLC's, which run the risk of a soiled reputation. The good news is there are steps you can take to sort it out.

Get in touch with a lawyer and consider the possibility of him or her writing the infringing business a cease-and-desist letter. If ever you'll have a lawyer do that, it's best to ensure that you were really the first one to use the trademark in question. If you make the mistake of going after an "infringing" company only to discover that the company you're complaining about was actually the first to use the trademark, it can boomerang on you when that business charges you back with the same accusation.

But even if you find yourself in such a situation, the good news is that you don't have to directly go to the courts. Most cases like these are settled amicably off-court and as such, your chances of having an amicable settlement and avoiding inconvenient and costly legal proceedings are high.

Top Business-Naming Mistakes to Avoid

Naming your LLC is akin to laying a building's cornerstone and once set, the building's entire structure and foundation is aligned with the cornerstone. Being misaligned by even just a small degree can throw the rest of the building off in terms of alignment. And if you have that inexplicable nagging feeling that choosing a good name for your LLC is crucial – you're right!

Choosing a great name involves 2 things: doing the right things and avoiding the wrong ones. We've already talked about doing the right things so now, we'll tackle the biggest mistakes you'll need to watch out for if you want to get this right. These are:

Too Many Chefs Can Spoil the Broth

While we live in a democratic society that espouses freedom and participation of the masses in deciding key issues, deciding on your LLC's name shouldn't be one of those key issues. Why? It's because this approach of involving your friends, family, relatives, neighbors, and even your friendly neighborhood newsboy can pose several problems.

First, you risk alienating people that you've involved. All of them will have their expert opinions on which name is best for your LLC and you can't pick them all! Well, unless you're ok with an LLC name that's about as long as a paragraph then that'd work really well.

The second possible problem you might encounter if you involve too many people is that you may just end up with a name that's too plain-vanilla or worse, lame. It's because you may want to decide through a consensus and doing so runs the very high risk of deciding on a relatively generic name that'll please most of the people you've consulted for the name.

The best way to do this would be to involve only a select few – the key people who'll be involved in making decisions for the LLC. This is a situation where the adage "the more the merrier" doesn't apply. Further, make sure to limit it to people who aren't just key to the LLC's success but to those who actually care about the LLC you'll be putting up. Oh, and don't involve people with egos as small as Mount Everest. Otherwise, it's going to be a long and tedious process, which may end up with you going for a name that you don't really like. Throw in some right-brained (creative) people in the mix. Too many left-brainers may lead to an LLC name that's a bit stiff, rigid or downright lame. You'll need a good serving of creativity to successfully come up with a good business name.

Forced Marriages

Forcibly marrying an adjective with a noun to come up with a uniquely sounding and great name for your LLC will only achieve in giving you a unique one that isn't great. Worse, it can even give you a uniquely sounding one that can ruin your LLC's reputation even before it's built.

How does a forced marriage look like? If you're putting up a professional LLC that aims to provide dental care, it would sound something like QualiDent (Quality Dental) or Dentacular (Dental and Spectacular). If you're organizing an LLC that is into operating a fitness gym, it'd sound like SpectaFit (Spectacularly Fit) or DeliFit (Deliciously Fit, ewe!).

Too Ordinary

If you'd like to establish your LLC as quickly as possible in the marketplace, make sure it'll get noticed. Using very ordinary words for your LLC's name will be able to help you do just that just as well as drinking a glass of water can help you look like Dwayne "The Rock" Johnson (for men) or Angelina Jolie (for women). Your LLC's name is the public's first point of contact with it and as such, you'll need to ensure it stands out in people's already overloaded and crowded minds.

Your LLC might get away with it if it's a pioneering business entity or there isn't any real competition in the industry. But if your LLC will be in a rather crowded market, a name that's too ordinary just won't cut it. In today's very competitive business world, your name has to be as unique and catchy as possible, which takes some effort to achieve.

Nationally Geographic

Many aspiring new entrepreneurs choose to name their businesses after the country, region, state or city in which they operate. While it's not especially harmful at the start, it can be in the future as the business grows.

Say for example your LLC will start operating mainly in Delaware. What if you decide to expand and operate in Miami? How's that going to sound in Miami, eh? Using a geographical name for your LLC can be quite limiting later on so it's best to avoid it whenever possible.

Consider some of the biggest companies who've made this mistake early on, which required the renaming or rebranding of their businesses to be more applicable to their new and larger markets. Have you ever heard of Minnesota Manufacturing and Mining Company? I doubt. How about 3M? Ah...yes! They had to rename the company when it started expanding beyond their state and industry. Same thing happened to Kentucky Fried Chicken, which is now known simply by its initials KFC.

Clichés

Another common mistake committed by many starting entrepreneurs when it comes to naming their businesses is turning them into clichés. After getting past descriptive and literal words, metaphors are next in line. If you don't overuse metaphors, they can be great name choices but use them too much that they become trite, they become more like liabilities instead of assets.

A good example would be businesses that view themselves as the best in their fields. Many such businesses use names that contain the words best, top, ultimate and others like it, which are too cliché already. The better alternative instead would've been to combine words like Iron Tower, which depicts height (of success) and strength and sounds unique.

Too Unique

While some businesses use names that are to plain and cliché-sounding, others go to the other extreme and use words that are too unique to the point of being obscure! While it's great if a business name is unique and conveys a particular significance or meaning that can help tell the story behind the company and its message, a business name whose words are too difficult to pronounce, and whose references are too obscure can keep your business from speaking and enticing customers because they simply don't get your business. It's too unique for customers to relate to and appreciate.

In this regard, resist the urge to name your business after some mythological character or exotic sounding phrase such as Mercury Laundry or Hakuna Matata Spa. Just don't, particularly if you want to reach as many customers as possible. Don't make your business name puzzling, complex and dumbfounding. Make it unique enough to be easily understood or appreciated.

Alternatively Uncool Spellings

Other business owners think it's cool to use names that are purposefully misspelled, as if the alternative spelling will sell better. Again...resist! Use proper spelling so you won't sabotage your chances. Avoid using names like KwaliKare (quality care), Kwik Eets (quick eats), Farmaceutika and others like it. Don't replace Qs with Ks and vice versa. Avoid substituting Fs with PHs and vice versa too. For the love of God!

Not that names that use terms that have been invented or coined won't work. They can and many have. Look at Kodak and Xerox. But consider one reason these worked – in and of themselves, those words didn't mean anything. They also relied on heavy advertising so consider the costs of doing the same. And if you look at it, some of the biggest businesses in the world committed this mistake and had to rebrand. If you don't believe me, ask Accenture and Verizon.

Holding On

Let's face it – everybody can make a mistake. When you make a mistake, the more important thing is to accept it, correct it and move on from it. The same goes with choosing a name for your LLC.

Many entrepreneurs choose the wrong business names for their enterprises. Many acknowledge their sins but do nothing to correct it. It's the same as not acknowledging at all. Somehow, they feel that the universe will just conspire to make things right if they but leave things be. But that doesn't happen. Mortals need to act and correct mistakes so that things will get better – including choosing a bad business name.

So as much as it's very exciting to choose a name for your LLC, don't leave your mind at the door. Take the time and effort to really think about coming up with a great name for both the long and short term. Always keep the image of a building's cornerstone in mind when coming up with a great name.

Keep in mind that choosing a bad name for your LLC shouldn't be the end of the world for you if you acknowledge the error and work on correcting it.

Now that you know how to create a name for your company and a few things you need to keep in mind let's move on to how to choose a tax type for your company; one of the most complex subjects when it comes to making a limited liability company.

Chapter 6 - Reviewing Tax Types for Limited Liability Companies

Because a limited liability company is allowed to choose pretty much any tax status that they want, the federal returns, information statements, and notices they have to file every year will vary depending on the status they choose. A limited liability company can choose the following types of taxation: partnerships, disregarded entity, S corporation, and corporation.

Let's go over these in a little more detail.

Disregarded Entity Taxation

This form of taxation is more like a default status for the single-member limited liability company. These types of limited liability companies don't qualify for partnership taxation because no partner exists, so they're automatically in this tax type unless they elect an S corporation or corporation tax status.

This form of taxation can be beneficial for some investment and real estate transactions. When a company is considered a disregarded entity through the IRS, the company is treated as if it's nonexistent and the company is treated as a sole proprietorship when it comes to taxation. This arrangement is beneficial for executing tax credits, strategies that apply to individuals, and deductions such as a mortgage interest deduction and special exception rule in a 1031 exchange of real estate.

Partnership

This is the default tax status for a limited liability company with more than one member. It's a form of pass-through taxation. The main benefit of partnership taxation over the other options is that assuming the primary intention is not tax avoidance, and then the company is able to vary the profit and loss allocations to the partners. In addition, recourse loans are deductible by the members who guarantee them.

Corporation

The corporate tax status differs greatly from all the rest. It's the non-pass-through form of taxation a limited liability company can choose. The revenues and expenses, and thus the losses and profits, of the company do not pass through to the members but are instead retained in the company and taxed at the corporate income tax rate. Because the corporation tax is usually lower than what the individual pays, this status can be beneficial in most cases.

In addition, when a member sells their interest in the company, the profit from that sale is subject to a favorable long-term capital gains rate. This can result in great tax savings. The major drawback, though, happens when normal profits are detached by members, producing a double-taxation situation.

S Corporation

This is the answer to a corporation's pass-through taxation conundrum. S-corporation tax status comes about when a small, closely held business needs the ability to operate under the liability protection of a corporation but without the heavy tax and regulation burden that comes with the usual corporation. Note that S-corporations are not an entity type but are just a tax election that can be made by either a corporation or a limited liability company.

The S-corporation's greatest benefit is that the members are able to hire themselves and pay themselves a salary. While the resulting tax burden is usually equal to the income tax and self-employment tax that they'd pay with partnership taxation, the members will only pay income tax on amounts that are over the salary they pay themselves, as in opposition to members who are answerable to partnership taxation who must pay self-employment tax and income tax on all the revenues over their wages. Obviously, you can't just pay yourself a dollar because the IRS demands that your salary be consistent with others in your industry and position.

Now that you know how to choose the proper type of taxation for your company let's look at the step by step instructions on how to actually form a limited liability company.

Chapter 7 – Accounting and Bookkeeping

An LLC is a state-authorized business entity. Despite being classified as neither a corporation nor a partnership, an LLC gives sole proprietors and business partners many of the benefits that come with being a corporation but without the extra operating and tax burdens. Putting up your LLC will entail you to manage several administrative aspects of your new business such as marketing, sales and more importantly, accounting.

Why Accounting?

You and your partners (referred to as members) can enjoy the same limited liability benefits as shareholders of corporations do. What this means is you and the other members are protected from particular types of financial risks such as your personal assets being seized in the event your LLC gets sued and convicted. But unlike corporations, your LLC will not be taxed.

Yes, LLCs aren't taxed, which does away with the hassles and burdens of you and the other members of being taxed twice. Record-keeping requirements such as those involving management and accounting aren't as stringent for LLCs unlike laws that govern corporations. Corporations are required to file annual reports in some states while LLCs aren't. As such, the annual and monthly accounting duties and responsibilities of LLCs are significantly simpler for you and the other owners.

Taxes

Even before establishing your LLC, you will need to first understand how both the state and federal governments tax different kinds of businesses. Doing so will help you file the right taxes in compliance with pertinent laws.

While you can learn and study about how you'll need to pay taxes on income derived from your LLC, it's best to consult with an expert tax professional instead. And while the IRS or the Internal Revenue Service doesn't tax LLCs, as mentioned earlier, your share of its revenues will be filed under your personal individual tax return. In most instances, you may also need to pay taxes as a self-employed individual.

General ledger

Besides taxes, LLCs accounting practices have much in common with other types of businesses. In this regard, the most crucial document that your LLC should maintain will probably be the general ledger. This will serve as the financial backbone of your LLC.

Just like how you – as an individual – keep a checkbook that records and documents every banking transaction you've ever executed, your LLC will utilize a general ledger to do the same when it comes to the money it will receive and spend daily. Apart from monetary assets like investments and cash, non-monetary ones like important pieces of office equipment and real estate are also included in your LLC's general ledger. Liabilities, which include lines of credit and loans, are also part of your LLC's general ledger.

The general ledger will give you the ability to audit and review each and every financial transaction that your LLC will carry out. And if your LLC is in in the industry that's highly regulated, this can be especially important.

How to Start Your LLC's Accounting and Bookkeeping Activities

The first step in starting your LLC's accounting and bookkeeping activities is determining its tax structure. Your LLC's tax structure is the determining factor in setting up your bookkeeping system for purposes of filing taxes. The most commonly used tax-filing form for LLCs is that of a partnership's because using it allows your LLC to enjoy pass-through taxation benefits. What this means is that revenues merely flow through your LLC to you and the other members who will only have to pay personal income tax on such income instead of business taxes that tend to be higher.

The second step is choosing a system or software to use for keeping the books of your LLC. Two of the most popular bookkeeping software for small businesses is Peachtree and QuickBooks because not only do they provide electronic means to monitor all of your LLC's transactions, they're also very simple to use. The bookkeeping system that you will eventually choose must be able to give you accurate income and expense statements every month as well accurate trial balance sheets on demand.

Next, you will need to create your LLC's chart of accounts, or COA. This should be consistent with the tax structure that you chose for your LLC. Your entire bookkeeping system will be based on your LLC's COA. Most bookkeeping software programs provide COAs that can be customized, which include basic accounts such as assets, liabilities, depreciation, capital expenditure, overhead and administrative expenses. Revenue accounts or assigned one kind of identification number while expenditure accounts are given a different one.

Next, you will need to categorize your COA's accounts based on the different kinds of expense and income items as well as how you'd like the reports to be presented. For example, you may like to group together your LLC's expense accounts into different categories like overhead expenses, cost of goods sold, and marketing expenses, among others. By doing so, this can help you prepare or generate reports that show each category's total amounts.

For the next step, you will need to input the names and addresses of your LLC's sales accounts to enable your system to automatically print sales invoices without doing extra work. You can come up with a template for such invoices and provide the first number of the very first invoice. Whenever you create invoices, the bookkeeping system will be the one to generate an incremental and unique number, add the sales amounts of each invoice to your LLC's total sales figures, and reflect the amount owed by the customer.

Next, you will need to set up the bank details of your LLC in the system. After setting it up, you'll have to insert your bank accounts' current balances. You'll also need to create a template for your checks that are aligned with and matches your LLC's checks. Input the check number of the very first check that your system will be printing. Whenever your LLC needs to make a payment, your bookkeeping or accounting system will be the one to automatically reduce your bank accounts balance, generate the subsequent check numbers, and print the required data on your LLC's checks.

As you approach the finish line of setting up your LLC's accounting and bookkeeping system, you will need to set up your LLC's taxes and payroll inside the system. Simply input the relevant details of your LLC's employees such as their employment starting dates, salaries (gross amount) and other factors like sick and vacation leave credits. Based on the details of your tax and payroll setup, your system will be the one to automatically determine the employee and payroll taxes as well as printing of salary checks every pay day.

Lastly, start recording all transactions of your LLC in your system. As you continue doing this, regularly reconcile your system's bank account totals with the actual bank statements. Doing this will help you be up to date in terms of your LLC's available funds, accounts payables and accounts receivables. Doing this will also allow you to get a good estimate of your LLC's projected tax returns for the year using its current income and expense totals, all of which can help you monitor your LLC's performance vis-à-vis its operating budget.

Common Bookkeeping Mistakes

Bookkeeping is a very important part of just about any type of business, from single person entities the big Fortune 500 corporations. Even if it is not one of the most interesting and prestigious jobs in your LLC, bookkeeping life the heart of its success and managing your LLCs bookkeeping erroneously may lead too serious losses and repercussions.

In order to avoid such repercussions and losses, consider the following errors that many businesses 10 to commit that you should be wary of:

- Not Keeping Receipts for Expenses Below $75: Even if the IRS doesn't require keeping such receipts, they can serve as important documentary support for tax deductions that you may want to claim. It's not very hard or complicated to keep a folder for keeping receipts of expenses that are less than $75, which may prove to be important later on for tax deductions purposes.

- DIY: Despite their professed disdain for handling their business's books, many owners of small businesses continue to insist doing it themselves. While it may cost a bit more to hire a competent bookkeeper, it will be well worth it. This is because competent bookkeepers are equipped with the necessary skills to efficiently and quickly handle your LLC's bookkeeping activities. They can also serve as an objective, second pair of eyes in terms of spotting bookkeeping errors or inconsistencies and giving suggestions for improvement in the bookkeeping process or the LLC's finances as a whole.

- Short Term Memory Loss: Often times, small business owners pay for their business's expenses out of their own pockets or by using their credit cards. And often times too, they forget to track such advances on behalf of their businesses. When this happens, the usually forget to submit such expenses for reimbursements to their businesses. This affects both the owner and their businesses because the owners tend to have an artificially higher level of personal expenses and the business tend to underestimate its own. So do yourself a favor and minimize the instances of making advances of behalf of your LLC. If possible, avoid it. You'll be doing yourself and your LLC a very big favor.

- Improper Employee Classification: The current proliferation freelancers, consultants and contractors gives many business owners a hard time figuring out who among the people working for them are their staff and who aren't. Often times, this results in wrong filing of taxes because tax rules and regulations for employees and non-employees are different.

- Insufficient Communications: Hiring a bookkeeper to handle your LLC's bookkeeping activities will only be beneficial and effective if they're up to date and are filled-in on all of your LLC's financial transactions. One of the most common mistakes in bookkeeping is giving an employee or a contractor a bonus or incurring other expenses that aren't forwarded to the bookkeeper in the form of necessary documents like invoices or receipts.

- Negligence in Reconciling the Balances for Bank Accounts: One very important part of bookkeeping for your LLC is regular reconciliation of balances between your LLC's bank account balances per its books and the actual bank statements that are sent to it every month. Oftentimes, this happens when business owners insist on doing the bookkeeping activities themselves. Hiring a competent bookkeeper can go a long way in terms of making sure your LLC doesn't commit this bookkeeping mistake.

- Not Backing Up: In the real business world, paperless businesses don't exist. However, audit processes and auditors still do. For auditors to do their jobs well, there must be established paper trails, verifications or documentations in the form of actual documents. Whether you like it or not, printed documents are still needed because there's always a risk that your electronic bookkeeping system may crash any time, rendering you or your LLC's bookkeeper unable to access financial data or worse, permanently lose them all. If you really must insist on paperless bookkeeping operations, make sure that you back up your electronic bookkeeping system's data daily and such backups are kept safe in a separate venue.

- Un-Deducted Sales Taxes: Another popular mistake small business owners make is not deducting the amount of sales tax from their total sales. What's the implication? The amount of taxes due on sales remains the same but total sales amount are artificially higher, which can be misleading.

- Lax Management of Petty Cash Funds: Many businesses take their petty cash funds for granted and as such, they become very lax in recording each and every time money is dispensed from it. In particular, it is very important to fill out duly approved petty cash slips with every withdrawal from the fund. This is because when the funds run out, all the slips' amounts will be added and should equal the initial or original amount before being replenished again. This ensures no unauthorized withdrawals were made. Many losses come about as custodians of petty cash funds become nonchalant about documenting petty cash withdrawals, which lead to unaccounted or unauthorized disbursements and consequently, losses.

- Wrong Categorization: Expense account categories are fairly standard but still, many businesses make the mistake of categorizing certain expenses erroneously. Oftentimes, expenses are lodged under the wrong categories or there are simply too many categories than are needed. Keep your categories as few as possible and be guided by general bookkeeping guidelines as well as follow generally accepted principles or practices for accounting.

Chapter 8 – Recap: Why operate as an LLC?

Are there some obvious advantages you have seen so far that would influence you to register as an LLC as opposed to other available choices? Obviously it is to your benefit if creditors cannot reach out to your personal assets the way they would in a partnership or sole proprietorship because of the limitation of your liability. That means you are able to expand your business through external borrowing because you can afford the risk. You are also at an advantage saving money by avoiding the double taxation investors experience in corporations. Generally, you will find yourself enjoying a lot of what both S-Corps and C-Corps enjoy, with more leeway to advance your ideas than in corporations. In short, as an LLC, you have the advantage of enjoying some benefits that sole proprietorships do; others that business partnerships do; and still others that a corporate enjoys.

What makes the LLC's position this convenient, you may wonder?

Simple – just look at the requirements of registering as an LLC. You can form an LLC even as you are – alone! For years, people particularly in the US have operated businesses alone but as single proprietorships. And the rate at which some of those businesses went down just when observers thought they were taking off was scaring. Now more people are daring to invest as individuals because they can have their liability limited even when they are singular owners of the business. You can also enjoy the protection of limited liability even when you are, for all practical purposes, operating as a firm of partners.

Here is a review of the advantages of operating as an LLC:

Tax advantage

In the eyes of the Internal Revenue Service (IRS), you are an entity made up of individual members or entities and so the IRS does not levy taxes on your organization and then levy taxes on your company profits. You enjoy what is termed Pass through Taxation. In fact, you have flexibility to make a choice in how you want your organization to be treated under the tax regime. For instance:

For your own reasons, you can opt to be treated as a corporation

You can also opt to be taken as a group of individuals with overall ownership; in which case each member reports his or her part of company income the way individuals in Sole

Proprietorships do – through their individual federal tax returns. Here it means that the LLC is not taxed as an entity.

You can also opt for members to be treated the way investors in a Business Partnership are treated.

When it comes to matters of accounting and taxation, consistency is paramount even as we speak of the legal position. So you need to have an operating agreement early on, which indicates how your LLC is going to be treated in taxation. Often, even the nature of your business can influence the choice you make in this regard. For instance, a number of companies rendering professional services, such as audit firms, opt to be treated as corporate.

So you find a PLLC filing a Form 1120S corporate tax return, where it shows its income for the year, expenses incurred in earning that income, as well as other business related items. With this application, the PLLC is treated as an S-Corporation. Other PLLCs choose to file Form 1120 where they make their income tax return, with taxation being levied at the normal corporate rate. Here it means that the PLLC has chosen to be treated as a C-Corporate for tax purposes.

Minimal Paperwork

Considering an LLC is taken to be a coming together of individuals, it means then that those same individuals can determine how their organization is going to be run. It is therefore easy to cut the bureaucracy found in corporate organizations that are largely regulated by stringent state laws. In short, you have more flexibility in decision making than when you are operating as either an S or a C corporate.

And primarily when it comes to matters of a statutory nature, LLCs are less bothersome. All you need after the initial registration of existence is the annual reporting plus the annual basic fee. Registration itself is simple. You file the mandatory articles of organization where you indicate your company name; whom your members are; your headquarters or location of your principal offices; and some other basic information that shows the nature of your business and related matters.

In comparison, when you are registering your entity as a corporation, you file Articles of Incorporation; hold corporate meetings where you elect your officers, make decisions regarding the share classes you should have, agree on and design by-laws to use in running your corporation; hold regular meetings of Board of Directors where discussions are held regarding business strategies and matters of finance, policy making and so on; and sometimes you even hold emergency or extra-ordinary meetings. You cannot also ignore the mandatory Annual General Meeting where the Board of Directors present the corporate status to the shareholders. And, of course, there is the usual filing of annual reports, payment of annual fees and such other statutory returns.

Limited liability

Nobody can attach your personal assets such as your home or vehicles because of a debt the LLC owes. The only assets that can be attached are those registered in the name of your company. So, as long as you have been operating within the law and you have not made any personal guarantees, say like personally guaranteeing a business loan, your assets are safe even when the company defaults on debt repayment.

Freedom in the manner of Profit Distribution

As an LLC, it is easy for you to make and uphold a decision not to distribute any profits the organization earns. And usually, this is not an arbitrary decision. Sometimes you may just find it prudent to plough back the profits into the business, for instance, to increase your production capacity. This should not come across as strange when you take into account that you can register an LLC with you as the sole investor. So you are not even obliged to consult the way partners do in a business partnership. And there is nothing binding you to stick to a certain way of profit distribution or retention.

Note how different this is from a partnership where profits are distributed as per the Partnership Agreement. However, in LLCs that are made up of many members, those that run almost like corporations, members normally stipulate the mode of distributing profits in the operating agreement of the LLC. And they can alter those terms whenever they deem fit. It is important to know that it is not obvious that profits in an LLC will be distributed in proportion to one's size of ownership or shareholding. Sometimes a member who has greater shareholding can receive the same profits as another with less if the other person volunteers to invest more time in the company's daily operations.

Of course even with all the freedom to distribute profits as the members wish there is no way an LLC is going to distribute profits and risk not meeting its legal and financial obligations. In any case, profits should be sufficient to cover liabilities as they fall due. And it is expected as a matter of common sense that an LLC will not dish out profits at the risk of insolvency, lest it risks the protection under limited liability being lifted by authorities or the company disintegrating.

Keeps things simple

The simplicity of an LLC does not end with its incorporation. It remains relevant even in the company's daily operations. Bureaucracy is less in LLCs than in corporations, which means that important investment decisions can be made faster making it easy for the organization to take advantage of sudden business opportunities. In the same vein, operational decisions can be made quicker making it possible to salvage an otherwise damaging situation. And when there is greater leeway to make decisions, the people involved feel a sense of ownership and responsibility for whatever happens to the organization. This is great for business.

All members have a say

Unlike in a partnership where you cease to participate in daily operations when you decide to take up limited liability, in an LLC every member has a right to participate fully and the liability for all of them is limited to the extent of their investment.

Capacity to build an independent credit history

As an LLC, the entity's credit history is independent of that of its individual members. So, whether some members are weak financially or not is not of any consequence to the business as what is important is that they are fully paid up members of the LLC. This means that a member who is personally struggling financially can continue earning and improving their personal life through the benefits of the LLC without anyone jeopardizing their position as stakeholders. Likewise, their personal liabilities cannot affect the company when it comes to business worthiness.

LLCs easily attract foreign investment

These days, people from Europe and other parts of the world find it easier to invest in the US since the country embraced the establishment of LLCs. And since LLCs have been a common phenomenon in other parts of the world, foreigners feel more at home investing through LLCs than through conventional corporations. This is important to company owners since one way of increasing capital when a company wants to expand its business is through increasing shareholding. And to the investing foreigners, they find it much safer to invest in LLCs than forming business partnerships with locals. In short, LLCs are more credible, stable and reliable than partnerships.

Chapter 9 – Step by Step Guide On How to Create a Limited Liability Company

It may seem daunting to organize an LLC at first glance but really, it's just an uncomplicated series of small, simple tasks. Here's how you do it in 10 steps.

Step One – Where Should You Organize?

The life of the LLC will formally start as soon as you and the other owners file its articles of organization with either the state's secretary or the department of state government that's is similar to such a position. The Federal Government doesn't charter LLCs.

There are a number of factors that you'll need to take into consideration prior to deciding where to best register your LLC, which include:

- The particular state/s you plan the LLC to operate in;

- The initial filing fees for your LLC;

- Filing fees paid annually as well as reports that need to be submitted annually; and

- Advantages particular to specific states, including privacy.

Generally speaking, if your planned LLC will be small and will operate in just one state or will be doing so mostly in that state, that's where you'll need to organize and register the limited liability company. But if your planned LLC will be operating in more than just a single state, you'll need to register it in all those states where you plan for it to operate. Different states will require your LLC to register as a "guest" and pay the necessary fees. If for example you want your LLC to be registered in Pennsylvania and do business in Delaware, you'll have to register in Delaware as well and pay a filing fee there too.

Choosing the place where you form your LLC can be as complicated as choosing its optimal legal structure. Basically, you have two options as to where you can register your LLC: domestic and foreign. If you choose to file as a domestic LLC, this means that your LLC will conduct its business in the same state in which you'll register it. On the other hand, choosing to file your LLC as a foreign one means that your LLC will also be doing business in other states aside from where you originally formed it.

All LLCs that conduct its business outside the states of their registration need to file what's called a "foreign qualification" so it can be allowed to do so in other states. Some of the things you may want to consider in choosing between filing as a foreign or domestic LLC include tax treatments, additional paperwork and disclosure and compliance obligations.

Most LLC owners choose to file their LLCs as domestic in their own home states. This is the most sensible choice if they transact most of their businesses at and if they're are physically located in the same state. For example, if you're running a retail store and most of your sales come from your home state, the logical thing to do is to file or register your LLC in that particular state. If you choose to file your LLC in a different state but run its store in the state where you are in now, you will need file it as a foreign LLC and pay the necessary additional fees that come with registering as such. As with other businesses, you'll have to comply with and pay both local and state laws, taxes and fees as well as dealing with added complexities, paperwork and costs of having to comply with mandates from another state. If you choose to have your LLC located in one state and its business transactions take place in the same state, filing as a domestic LLC is the easier and more cost-efficient way to go.

Some startups however plan to do business in multiple states outside their own. If your planned LLC will focus on out-of-state business transactions, your LLC will definitely benefit from being registered as a foreign one. Still, the best thing to do is to consult with a competent tax professional or lawyer to determine whether or not filing as a foreign LLC would be beneficial to you and your partners. And if you considered filing as a foreign LLC, three of the best states to consider are Delaware, Nevada and Wyoming, all of which have a stellar reputation of being conducive places for LLCs.

Delaware

As a state, Delaware has a reputation of being business-friendly with more than half of all companies that are publicly-traded in the United States and as much as 63% of all Fortune 500 companies having been incorporated in this state. Consider too that statutes governing the formation of LLCs are very progressive and accommodating plus, they're filing fees are quite low. For foreign LLC's that operate in Delaware, no corporate income taxes are levied. In addition, franchise taxes in Delaware are low. You also don't need to fulfill residency mandates to register your LLC in Delaware and you can also benefit from its limited disclosure and reportorial requirements.

The state also has a special court that's dedicated for businesses-related cases, which is called the Delaware Court of Chancery. It has more than two centuries of experience when it comes to settling business disputes as well as interpreting laws that govern businesses activities. Their Division of Corporations is also known to be efficient and fast with giving public service.

Nevada

Nevada is another state that is considered to be very friendly, with laws that are considered to be favorable for businesses. Just like Delaware, the judicial system in Nevada is perceived to be very friendly to businesses. Further, Nevada doesn't have franchise taxes, personal income taxes or corporate income taxes and the state doesn't share information with the IRS.

As an owner of an LLC, you can enjoy the benefits of not being named in public registration filings of your LLC in Nevada. Further, the state doesn't mandate or call for annual or organizational meetings and doesn't require you or your LLC to have an operating agreement.

Wyoming

As with the two other states mentioned earlier, Wyoming is also a business-friendly state. It only requires minimal reporting and annual meetings may even be held outside the state. As with Nevada, Wyoming doesn't levy any franchise, personal income or corporate income taxes.

Wyoming also gives you the benefit of privacy in terms of not being identified as the owner of your LLC in public records. Further, the state allows you to use lifetime proxies, which allow you to protect your identity as well as your assets by authorizing other people to hold and exercise the prerogatives that come with your membership shares while keeping control of your voting rights when it comes to deciding on your LLC's strategies, policies and other important matters.

Step Two – The Name

At this point, you'll need to choose your LLC's name. Bear in mind that you can use a different trade name in the market from your LLC's actual or registered name. If you choose to use different names for trade and business, that's known in the industry as DBA or doing business as a fictitious name. An example of this would be a store named Powerlift while your LLC's registered business name is Powerlifting Systems Limited Liability Company. Your single biggest consideration – legally speaking – is is that your chosen name must be one that no other person or business is already using and this particular consideration is influenced by two factors:

1. The company name you choose for your LLC mustn't infringe on another's service mark or trademark rights because doing so can get your LLC in a whole lot of trouble.

2. The office of the Secretary of your chosen state will never allow a new limited liability company to register under the exact same name under which an existing LLC is already registered. Keep in mind though that your chosen state's Secretary's office only keeps records of such for that particular state only. If you want to make sure that the name you'd like to register your LLC with won't infringe on the rights of another LLC from another state, you'll need to do your homework and you can't just rely on the verification of your particular state's Secretary's Office.

When checking out the state secretary's records of currently existing names of LLCs or other companies, you must search an online database that contains such information with the state secretary of the state where you plan to register or organize your planned LLC in. Remember your chosen name for your LLC can be distinguished from other LLCs and other business entities. Fortunately, almost all state secretary websites feature search tools that you can freely use to verify.

Lastly, your LLC's name must include identifiers as such like Limited Liability Company, LLC or Limited Liability Co. For example, Powerlifting Systems Limited Liability Company, LLC or Limited Liability Co.

Step Three – Find a Registered Agent

Registered agents are people or business entities that your LLC can authorize and obligate to receive legal documents on its behalf. Because your LLC isn't a real, physical person, it would be quite impossible for it to be served legal documents as an LLC. Your LLC's registered agents are identified in its articles of organization but you can always replace your registered agent simply by filing a notice with the state's secretary. It's possible that other states where you're considering to organize your LLC may use a different term to refer to registered agents so include it as part of your research on the states you're eyeing for your LLC.

Your LLC's agent may be a member of your own family, yourself, a designated officer, another member of your planned LLC, a lawyer, or another person or company that provides professional registered-agent services. The agent's name must be publicly recorded and so if you'd like to enjoy anonymity, you must choose a professional registered agent for this purpose.

The registered agent needs to have an actual, physical address in the same state where you'll organize your LLC. So if your LLC won't operate in the state where you'll register it in, you'll also have to hire a registered agent for that particular state where you organized it. Given the additional expenses related to such, it would do you well to think doubly hard whether or not to organize outside your state of business operations.

If you're totally clueless as to where to hire a registered local agent, you can check out www.bizfilings.com, a website offers professional services of resident local registered agents in all of the 50 states in the US.

Hiring a lawyer or a professional services firm for this purpose offers several advantages. As the registered agent's primary role is to receive legal documents on behalf of your LLC, the lawyer or firm will need to have a permanent address and will need to be very well versed in such documents that will be served to you. Also, the registered agent you'll hire for your LLC will be responsible for important Federal and State-related documents like legal notices, tax forms, and annual report forms, among others.

Take note that most of the offices of the secretaries of states where you can organize your LLC won't be particular whether or not you've contracted the services of such an agent. However, if you don't choose a good registered agent for your LLC, you run the risk of either not receiving important legal documents or handling such poorly, both of which can significantly affect your LLC's state of good standing with the state government.

Qualifications of Your LLC's Registered Agent

More than just being consistent, accurate and reliable, your LLC's registered agent must be:

- Physically present and always available at your LLC's registered office on regular business hours to ensure that important legal documents that are hand delivered to are properly attended to.

- Be knowledgeable of the compliance and business entity rules of the state where it's operating because each state has different rules, regulations and laws.

- Knowledgeable about all types of business entities like LLC's, corporations and partnerships, among others.

- An expert in the area of compliance management. Your registered agent must be professional and have the necessary resources to make sure that your LLC's able to comply with all state laws, regulations and mandates. Many professional service companies can give you a complete range of registered-agent services and as such, it may be a good idea to get their services, if your budget permits.

A good professional services firm can help ensure your LLC's compliance and proper handling of documents. Typically, full service registered agent services:

- Make use of automated monitoring services and tools;

- Keep you up-to-date on new compliance procedures as they are issued;

- Immediately notify you if your good standing with authorities has changed in order for you to properly address any problems as soon as possible;

- Continuously track and monitor developments, changes and compliance events state-by-state; and

- Alerts your LLC of any changes.

One area where a registered agent can provide valuable help to your LLC is in the area of filing annual reports. If ever your LLC fails to file its annual report on time, if the state where it's operating requires such, your LLC's good standing status may be jeopardized and that will need immediate action to address the problem. Employing a competent registered agent will help you file your annual reports on time every time.

Another service a good registered agent may provide, which you may not want to need, is called Service of Process or SOP. Your LLC's registered business address is where your State's Sheriff will normally deliver the SOP papers related to lawsuits filed against your LLC. And when this undesirable event happens, engaging the services of a good registered agent – who is professionally trained and equipped with expert knowledge – can help you properly handle such documents. And because good a registered agent has to be physically present in your LLC's registered business address during operating hours, you're assured that you won't miss out on any important documents delivered to your office.

Step Four – *Organize it yourself or Hire an Attorney?*

At this particular point of your LLC creation process, you'll have to decide already whether you'll file and organize your planned LLC by yourself, hire a lawyer or get the services of a discount limited liability service company. Each of the 3 approaches has its pros and cons.

Self-Organization

Obviously, one of the benefits of doing it yourself is cost savings. Because you don't have to pay a lawyer or a company to do the dirty work for your, you save a lot of money – well at least in the beginning. Unless you're an established expert in this matter or have extensive experience with such, you may end up spending more later on as you fix problems or complications that may arise due to your lack of expertise and knowledge of the process. For example, if you poorly and incorrectly organized your LLC, you may fail to enjoy the limited liability protection a properly organized LLC gives to its members and your LLCs creditors may be able to go after your personal assets in the future as settlement for the LLC's unpaid debts.

Discount LLC Organization Services

This is a better – but more expensive – alternative to the DIY approach we discussed earlier. Availing of such services will only set you back about $300 and you'll be able to enjoy competently streamlined LLC organizing services. These firms can provide you with the following services, among others:

- Filing of your LLC's articles of organization with the correct state secretary's office;

- They'll take care of preparing your LLC's boilerplate operating agreement; and

- Minutes-taking for your LLC's first membership meeting.

Such service organizations can provide some value for your money. Among them is the convenience – you won't have to go through various technicalities and hassles of dealing with different states – as well as the assurance that your LLC's organization will handled correctly and significantly faster than if you did it yourself. But given that they're considered "discount services", the boilerplate agreement and proposed templates for taking minutes of your LLC's meetings may be a bit challenging to understand if you're just new to the game.

Hiring an Experienced Business Attorney

The final option is to engage the services of a business lawyer to help you in organizing your LLC. He or she will provide you with the following services:

- Alternatives and solutions that will optimize your LLC organizing success;

- Assistance for the relatively technical and complex aspects of organizing your LLC such as operating agreements and manager-managed LLC organization;

- Proactive management of risks related to your LLC's organization;

- Preparation of the minutes of your LLC's organizational meetings as well as its operating agreement in accordance with your LLC's specific needs; and

- Ensuring your LLC's consistent compliance with applicable laws and regulations, especially when it comes to raising capital for your LLC.

The cost of hiring a good business lawyer varies greatly but on average, a good business lawyer's hourly rate ranges from $100 to about $400. You can expect the scope and quality of service to be generally much better from lawyers whose hourly rates are on the upper range compared to those on the lower ranges. But for purposes of organizing your LLC, business lawyers normally charge flat rates, which may be as low as $500 to as high as $2,000 for complete and comprehensive LLC-organization package.

Step Five – Determine the LLC Ownership

Your LLC will need to issue shares of ownership called "units" to you and the other members, which is an integral part of its organization. Each member's units in the LLC are collectively referred to as their percent of ownership or interest in the LLC. For example, if your LLC will issue 100 units to you and the other members and you get 60 of those 100 units, then your interest or ownership percentage is 60%. Your LLC must do this from the get go and you shouldn't proceed with filing its articles of organization until this process has been completed.

One of the main rights of each member is the right to vote, the extent of which is dependent on how much of the LLC they own or have an interest in. Let's go back to the previous example of you owning 60 units. This means you, as a member of the LLC, are entitle to 60 votes out of a total 100 votes. It doesn't mean you'll have to vote 60 times though. It simply means that your vote counts for 60 votes in accordance with the number of units you of the LLC you own. With more units or percentage interest/ownership comes more control over the LLC. In our example, you control the company having majority share and votes.

How Many Members?

During the early days of LLC's in the United States, states compelled them to have multiple members, i.e., single-member LLC's weren't allowed. That isn't the case anymore as all states in the US the organization and operation of single-member LLCs, which shouldn't prohibit you from putting up one all by yourself!

On the other end of the spectrum, there isn't any limit as to how many members your LLC may have. Well, actually there is – your desired limit. In other words, it's you – and other members – who'll decide how many to admit into the LLC. And while you have complete autonomy in this, this is another area where the adage "the more the merrier" isn't applicable. There are cases where more is better – especially when it comes to equity financing – and there are instances where fewer is the way to go, where control and ease of deciding on key matters regarding the LLC are concerned.

Each member of your LLC – including you – must provide what is called an investment representation letter, which gives the LLC a good level of assurance that each member is qualified and fit to be a member. Also, this letter will require the member concerned to disclose their objectives for investing in the LLC in accordance with securities laws of the Federal and state governments.

Members can also contribute capital or invest in your LLC via non-cash assets such as properties, services, and receivables, among others. The monetary value of these will determine how much interest or ownership it will have in the LLC. Such values must be determined and agreed upon as early as the planning stage in order to avoid complications and issues later on, which may snag the LLC's organization process. Agreements concerning the monetary values of such contributions must be clearly detailed in the LLC's operating agreement.

Step Six – File the Articles of Organization

Your LLC comes to life as soon as you and other members file the articles of organization, which is normally just a single page document that outlines, among other things, the following:

- The LLC's name;

- The registered agent's name and address for purposes of handling SOPs and receiving legal documents for the LLC;

- Statement of your LLC's reason for existence or purpose;

- Names of your LLC's initial members or designated officers or manager; and

- Other important stuff like its expected life, i.e., whether it will continue indefinitely or be dissolved at a particular date, and how dissolution of the LLC will be managed.

As mentioned earlier, your LLC starts to come to life by filing its articles with office of the secretary of the state where you plan to organize and register your LLC. When filing the articles, you'll have to file a fee, which varies depending on the state you're organizing in.

In most cases, your LLC's initial members or appointed managers don't have to be appointed immediately in the articles that you'll file – unless of course the state you're organizing your LLC actually requires it. Some states that require this include Nevada and California. This is yet another reason why DIY-ing it may not cut it for you and why you'll need to do your homework really well or hire an expert to take care of it for you. It may be the case that you've organized an LLC in one state but because there are still differences in the laws and regulations on LLCs of each and every state, you may still be considered a rookie if you organize another LLC in another state.

Your LLC's additional members and managers can be elected without hassle even after filing. Your LLC's articles of organization are considered to be documents of public nature and as such, any citizen of that particular state can look it up to know the names of its members, save for a few states that offer privacy benefits.

Just about every website of the office of every states' secretaries provide samples or templates of the articles of organization that need to be filed in their jurisdictions that you can easily adapt for your LLC's filing. With these resources, you'll be able to cut down the amount of time and hassle involved in filing your LLC's articles by having a good idea of how your LLC' articles should look like and what are the things that need to be included in it.

Step Seven – Order the LLC Kit and Seal

Your LLC's kit is simply a binder that will be used to store its important documents such as its articles or organization, operating agreement, meetings' minutes, tax filings, licenses and membership log, among other things that are crucial for its compliance with Federal and state laws. The kit can cost around $50 to $100, which normally includes:

- A sample or template of minutes of the organizational meeting as well as of the operating agreement, together with provisions;

- Stock certificate forms (blank certificates);

- Unfilled membership and transfer logs or ledgers;

- An LLC embossed seal; and

- Soft copies of the many forms your LLC will need to accomplish stored in a compact disc.

Keep in mind that these kits aren't mandatory per Federal and state laws – they're optional. Since you're going to be preparing and filing such important documents for your LLC, might as well use such kits to make it easier for you to prepare, file and organize them well.

LLC Seal

Your LLC's seal is an embossing seal that's manually operated. It embosses your LLC's name, the state in which it's organized or operating in as well as its organization date on official documents such as your LLC's minutes of meetings, among others. The LLC seal is a direct descendant of the corporate seal and was once mandatory for all LLCs to have in all states. These days however, it's usually not required of LLCs.

Stock Certificates

These are basically printed documents that show a member's ownership of units in your LLC and your LLC kit includes blank forms of these that you can use to make your own. You can print the details on your LLC's certificates either manually, using a typewriter (if they still exist) or running them through your printers.

In the past, stock certificates were linked purely to corporations. These days however, they're also used for LLCs, who tend to operate with much less formality and complications than corporations. While limited liability companies don't normally use stock certificates, you can greatly benefit by using such for yours as these give your members a written evidence of their interest or ownership in the LLC.

Membership Log or Ledger

These are basically tables or log sheets that present the current owners or members of your LLC as well as their respective percentage of ownership or interest in relation to the total. As new members are added via purchase of existing member's interests or shares in the LLC, the logs or ledgers are updated to reflect their ownership or interest in the LLC as well as the reduced ones of the members from whom they bought their shares or interest. Any transfers or additions of interest or ownership in the LLC must be recorded in the membership log or ledger, including those resulting from death of members or issuance of new shares or interests in the LLC.

You can never overemphasize the importance of the membership log or ledger and as such, your LLC must be very consistent and diligent in maintaining it and ensuring it's kept current. Consider this log or ledger like the deed or title to a property, i.e., it's the primary evidence of interest or ownership in your LLC and as such, can be used in court to settle ownership disputes. To minimize such disputes, it's best to either issue certificates to your members or provide them with latest copies of the log or ledger as they're updated.

Step Eight – Choose Managers and Define the Management Structure

Next, you'll need to decide whether or not your LLC will be one that's managed by members (member-managed) or will you hire a professional manager to run it (manager-managed). Your choice of management structure won't be carved in stone as your LLC can without restrictions – other than those you and the members impose – shift from one type to the other, i.e. member-managed to manager-managed and vice-versa, through a membership voting and amendment or revision of its operating agreement.

Essentially, you and the other members will be the one to operate your LLC much like a partnership, if you decide it to be one that's member-managed. In most cases, smaller LLCs are member-managed because among other things, managing a small LLC in this manner doesn't need voting or appointing managers. The members simply buckle down to work. In almost all cases, single-member LLCs are member-managed, too.

On the other hand, making your LLC a manager-managed one will require you to appoint professional managers to run it like a corporation or a limited partnership. While it can make life easier for you and the other members in terms of running your LLC's daily operations, they can make your lives a bit more complicated in another way. In particular, you and the other members (unless you're a single-member LLC) to vote when appointing or removing managers, not to mention you'll need to formalize rules that will govern such activities. Normally, large LLCs are manager-managed due to the size and complexity of their operations as well as their deeper pockets.

If you and the rest of your LLC's members agree to make yours a manager-managed one, you'll need to set some important things straight at the onset. One of these is how many professional managers will your LLC need to hire to run it? The bigger your LLC is, the more managers you'll need to run it due to increasing scope and complexity of operations.

Another thing to discuss in terms of the number of managers to hire is whether or not to hire odd-numbered or even-numbered managers. In most cases, odd-numbered management teams are preferred simply because there can be no deadlocks when it comes to making decisions and getting their consensuses on important matters. With even-numbered management teams, your LLC runs the risk of deadlocks, which can involve members' intervention as well as the court's, in worst case scenarios.

After you and your members decide on your LLC's management structure as well as how many managers to hire, if any, you'll need to choose the most appropriate provision for its operating agreement. If your LLC is to be a manager-managed one, you'll have to choose your initial set of managers at the onset and identify them in your operating agreement. Keep in mind that the managers you choose to run your LLC need not be a member but they can be so too.

At the end of the day, the managers you choose will and should be at the service of you and all the other members of the LLC. As such, ensure that the operating agreement you and the other members will formalize must provide clear and distinct provisions for managing managers, especially in terms of replacing them when they're not performing up to par. It would also do your LLC good to rotate or change your managers every so often, say every other or every few years. This is because indefinite appointments can lead to potential problems like familiarity, complacency or worse, a sense of entitlement.

Step Nine – Prepare and Approve the Operating Agreement

Your LLC's operating agreement is what will be the basis for how it will conduct its business, including how meetings will be conducted, what constitutes a "quorum", how voting procedures will be conducted, the rights and powers of members and managers and elections. Normally, operating agreements are anywhere from 5 to 25 pages. And if you have no idea how to go about making one, getting an LLC kit (as mentioned earlier) can be of great help as it provides a sample or template for an operating agreement. The agreement need not be filed with your LLC's state of organization or operations and these are confidential and comprise part of your LLC's important records or documents.

You and the other members will need to put in the time and effort to come up with a very good operating agreement, even if you have the benefit of being guided by a sample or template from your LLC kit. As the name suggests, such are only samples or templates and the nitty-gritty of the important details are still yours and the other members' responsibility. Make sure that before finalizing it and enforcing it, all the members – including you – have read through it carefully and understand it fully. It's easier to modify now rather than later when it's already set, which will need membership voting.

Even if many states don't require this document, it's not wise to operate your LLC without one. The reason is very simple: if agreements aren't documented, they can be open to a lot of misunderstandings or even misrepresentations because there's no documentary and objective evidence that can be used to settle disputes. With a formal operating agreement, disputes and disagreements can be kept to a minimum because there's minimal room for subjectivity.

If the members don't use an operating agreement, the limited liability company will be governed by the state's default regulations and rules. The default rules are set out in every state's statutes. Naturally, they don't cover every possible circumstance that could arise. They just cover the basics. You shouldn't rely on the default regulations because they might not be the right ones for your company.

Lastly, using an operating agreement can protect the members from personal liability in connection with the business. Members should always try to give the limited liability company a separate existence, to hold the limited liability company out to the public. A limited liability company without a written operating agreement will appear more like a sole proprietorship or partnership. Limited liability companies require a lot fewer formalities than corporations, but that doesn't mean they require none at all.

Percentage of Ownership

One of the most important decisions the owners of the company will face is how the ownership percentages are divided amongst the members. Choose wisely. In most cases, more than fifty percent of the vote of a limited liability company's members can dictate significant decisions within the limited liability company. This is why many company founders will try to get fifty-one percent ownership in order to maintain control over the company. In addition, if the limited liability company is ever sold, the money received will be divided amongst the owners in proportion to their ownership.

The owners' percentage ownership should be written down as part of the operating agreement. The written record will get rid of any later misunderstandings or disputes pertaining to the share of ownership.

Distributive Share

The distributive share is the owner's percentage share of the limited liability company losses and profits. Usually, a member's distributive shares will equal their percentage of ownership shares. This is how most will set up their limited liability company. For example, let's say Jane has fifty-five percent ownership and Joe has forty-five percent ownership of the company. At the end of the year, they have profits of $20,000 divided between them as owners. They'll divide the profits according to the ownership share. Jane will receive fifty-five percent or $11,000 and Joe will receive forty-five percent or $9,000.

The operating agreement will cover the following items:

- The duties and powers of the managers and members

- The date and time of the annual meetings that the members and managers will get together

- Procedures for removing a manager if one exists

- Procedures for electing a manager

- Minimum requirements for the member votes

- Minimum requirements for the manager votes

- Procedures for voting with written consent without appearing at a formal meeting

- Procedures for giving proxy to the other members

- How profits and losses will be divided amongst members

- Buy-sell rules which will define the procedures for transferring when a member wants to sell their interest or they die

The owners of the company formally adopt the operating agreement through signing the agreement and agreeing that it will run the operation of the limited liability company. An operating agreement is a contract amongst the members of the company; once it's been executed, the limited liability company's members are bound by the terms.

Step Ten – Obtaining a Federal Tax Identification Number

Because the limited liability company is a legal entity, the federal government requires that the company has its own Federal Employer Identification Number (FEIN). Also, most banks will require that you have an EIN before you open a bank account for the limited liability company. Here are the steps to get an FEIN in for your LLC.

First, go to the website of the IRS at IRS.gov then type in the website's search box "EIN". A link that says "Apply Online Now" will appear and when it does, click on that link. It will take you to the webpage where you can read instructions on how to get an FEIN and on that same page, click on the "Begin Application" button and click on "Limited Liability Company" when the web page asks you identify your business' structure. Then, provide the necessary information on the nature of your LLC's business activities and its number of employees.

Next, you can call 800-829-4933 in order to talk to an IRS business and tax line representative. Keep your LLC's information nearby in order for you to easily answer the questions that may be asked by the representative. If you'll assign a representative to do this, the representative must provide an address, a name and social security number. And after the IRS representative verifies the given information, your LLC will get its FEIN that it can use immediately 4 business-related purposes.

Next, download form S-4 from the website of the IRS and print it. Only after printing the form can you type in the information or write such using a pen. The form must also be signed by your LLC's authorized representative, which can either be you, another member or the designated manager. After filling up the form, fax it to 859-669-5760 if your LLC is located in the United States. If it's not, you can fax the form to 215-516-1040. You must provide the IRS with a return fax number to which it can send your LLC's FEIN.

Alternatively, you can mail the form instead of faxing it to Internal Revenue Service EIN Operation Cincinnati, OH 45999. This particular address is only for LLCs that have a US business office. And for LLCs that don't have a US office, the forms must be mailed to Internal Revenue Service EIN International Operation Philadelphia, PA 19255.

Lastly, you can also get your FAA n number using a third-party service. However, you will need to pay a fee for it.

The Fiscal Year

Limited liability companies must have the same fiscal year-end as the members. While they can have corporations as owners, it's more common for the limited liability company to be owned by a real person. A real person has a fiscal year that ends on December 31st. Therefore, the limited liability company's tax returns are due on April 15th the following year.

Once you have all that together and everything filed and sorted, you have a limited liability company!

Chapter 10 – The Responsibilities and Rights as Member of an LLC

Being part of an LLC is really a great thing in business for reasons of investment and security, but have you thought of your responsibilities as an individual member or part owner of the LLC? Just as a shareholder in a corporation has obligations, you too have yours as part of an LLC. Of course you also have rights that include sharing in the company profits. Sometimes you may be required to take part in the daily running of operations depending on your agreement as members, and sometimes you may be called upon to make crucial decisions in collaboration with other members.

You need to remember the flexibility that an LLC accords its members, so that although you become a member usually by contributing some amount of money, it is not strictly the sole method. You could still become a member with rights as any other member by contributing tangible assets during the company formation stage. You could also be accepted as a member by you contributing your professional expertise or any other valuable intangible property. Even promissory notes are acceptable if the other members so agree. And there is no restriction as to what contribution you can make when founding an LLC for you to become a founder member.

Actually when you want to know your LLC's position as far as admission of a new member is concerned, the place you need to fall back to is the LLC's operating agreement. Usually there is the mention that the other members need to be in concurrence in deciding to accept a new member. The operating agreement also stipulates the acceptable consideration a new member has to provide in order to be accepted into the LLC – its form and amount, size or magnitude, depending on what it is. Likewise, the operating agreement stipulates the terms of suspension or expulsion as a member of the LLC. If your LLC's operating agreement is not clear or does not address any of those pertinent issues, then you are expected to rely on the LLC act.

Here are the main rights of a member:

Rights on finances

The reason you acquire ownership interest in the LLC is that you get to share in the company profits. Also when it is time to distribute tangible assets, you also partake of that as a right. And that position holds true whether the business is a going concern or whether it is preparing to wind up.

Just as a reminder, it is important to mention that the extent to which your right to share in profits or assets goes is based on the LLC's operating agreement. And again, if that one doesn't stipulate the modalities of sharing, then as members of the LLC, you are bound by the state laws that have default standard criteria.

Voting rights

Every member has a right to vote on virtually every aspect of the business as long as the LLC is member managed. And you may be wondering if there are different forms of management – yes, there are: member managed and one based on the management of professional managers. What this means is that you can choose to manage your LLC on your own as members or owners, and then you have a say on how day to day operations are carried out; the manner of handling business; strategic plans; and virtually everything else affecting the company. Of course, this situation may be a bit different if your LLC allows different form of membership, including non-voting membership. And if this is the case, it will be stipulated in the LLC's operating agreement. In such an instance, any member without voting rights will, definitely, not engage in voting.

However, if your LLC is manager driven, your power to vote as members will be limited to the most crucial; like admission of a new member; matters involving mergers; amendments to the operating agreement; amendments to the articles of organization; matters relating to dissolution; and such other weighty matters. Of course, when it comes to engaging or terminating the services of the company managers the members will have a say too, but when it comes to what actions to take regarding the business operations, it is left to the managers.

Inspection of company records

There are many states that demand that an LLC maintain specific records and that those records be available for members to inspect them at will. The basic records often include:

- List of names of the current members of the company

- The addresses of the current members of the company

- Copies of tax returns for the three most recent consecutive years; both federal and those for the state of business operation

- A copy of the company operating agreement in its current, updated form

- The LLC's financial statements for the three most recent consecutive years

For some states that do not explicitly state that an LLC maintains records for members to inspect, they often point out the need to keep records for the sake of availing them to members to facilitate them perform the duties they are meant to perform on behalf of the company. And of course in situations where the operating agreement and other documents are not clear, the LLC statute becomes the default document to adhere to.

Right to dissent
This right involves you refusing to accept a form of ownership that you did not sign for in the first place; the

changing of the character of your interest in the company. Say your LLC entered a merger agreement with another without you being consulted and without you being in concurrence with the move – you have a right to demand that the company buys back your interest in the company. And the company should actually buy back your interest at a reasonable value.

Examples of other developments that may prompt you to dissent include the company selling off the whole lot of their assets or even the company changing from the LLC that you formed to another form of entity. It is, however, important to note that not all states spell out the right to dissent in their acts. Others simply give indication that you can include that right in your LLC's operating agreement.

Filing of a derivative suit
Making a derivative suit encompasses you initiating a suit against people within or outside the organization who are messing with the company; putting it at a disadvantage or in jeopardy. As you are making this suit on behalf of the LLC, if the court rules in your favor, it means that the LLC has won. As such, any damages awarded by the courts go directly to the company. In order for your suit to be valid, here are some conditions you must fulfill:

You must have been a member of the LLC during the time the damaging actions were done against the company

You must have attempted to get the company itself to sue; only you did not succeed

It is important to note that in some states, the LLC act does not provide for a member's right to derivative suit. In such instances, you need not get discouraged from fighting for your company. Depending on what your state laws are like, you may still be able to sue under common law. And if that is not an option, then you can proceed with the suit and let the courts of law make their decision on how to handle the situation in the interest of the company.

Right to compensation

If your LLC is member managed, which means you are all meant to take part in managing the affairs of the company, if you actively do the running of the business on behalf of the others or more than them, then you have a right to be compensated commensurately or in a manner to keep you motivated. These are some of the stipulations you may often find in the operating agreement.

Right of disassociation

You have the right to leave the LLC any time as long as you adhere to the procedure provided for in the operating agreement. However, in case you disassociate from the company contrary to the provisions of the operating agreement, you may be slapped with liability against the company.

Here are the main obligations of a member:

Managing the LLC

If your company is member managed, you are obliged to take active part in running its affairs. If as you form the LLC you decide to do the management yourselves and then you realize the work is too much for you to handle, you could amend your operating agreement as members to prescribe employment of managers.

Fair and lawful distribution of profits and assets

The operating agreement stipulates how the LLC is expected to distribute its profits and any other benefits. You are obliged to keep to it. Of course, if majority of you think there needs to be change, it is allowed. However, if you ever vote to conduct such distribution in a manner that is illegal, you will be personally liable.

Fiduciary duty to the LLC

This aspect is mainly emphasized for members of an LLC who are also managers of the same LLC. Such a member must take care not to breach his or her fiduciary duties to the company. Every member is also expected to respect the provisions of the operating agreement.

And even after a member has left the company, if the operating agreement contains a non-compete clause, the member who has disassociated from the company has fiduciary duty to the company not to sabotage its business activities.

Bearing a proportionate amount of loss

The same way every member has a right to share in company profits, so are they obliged to share in its losses. Of course the operating agreement spells out how to go about the sharing.

Taking up losses

Whenever the company makes losses, every member suffers the loss to the extent of their membership interest in the LLC. So, even when it comes to liquidation of assets and dissolution of the company, you cannot expect to receive your full contribution back if the company liabilities exceed its assets.

Chapter 11 – Dissolving an LLC

Why is dissolution of an LLC a big deal? Well, it is a big deal because just as you followed a laid down procedure to establish your LLC for a reason, there are worthy reasons why you need to follow some defined procedure to wind it up. As you may recall, you did not wake up one morning to declare yourself an LLC. There were matters of registration, issues of capital and so on. Again, as an LLC, you are answerable as a legal entity and not as individual members who form it. So you need to give opportunity to all stakeholders, having in mind that they are not all members of your LLC, to have their say if they need to.

In fact, you may find dissolving an LLC a little more challenging than your experience establishing it. This is understandable considering that often you begin your LLC on a clean slate but there is likely to be some mess to clean up by the time you decide to wind it up. And by mess we mean legal, financial or such other business related issues.

It is important to mention here that dissolving an LLC is sometimes referred to as cancellation of the LLC. That is why you may here some people talking of Articles of Cancellation when they are referring to the Articles of Dissolution. Anyway, before you get to the actual resolution, here are a few things you must adhere to:

Vote

Unless you are a one-person LLC, you must consult before taking a step as drastic as dissolving your company. So meet with the other members and vote on the proposal to dissolve your organization. For the resolution to dissolve to pass, members who vote for it need to have a greater total shareholding compared to those who vote against it. In some states, a unanimous agreement does just fine. Still, you need to take into account what your operating agreement stipulates.

Draft the resolution

Have you agreed to dissolve the company? Yes. But think about it – that yes could turn into a no if some members with dissenting voices begin to lobby others who were for it earlier on. The impact...? You may be said to be acting unilaterally, contrary to the stipulation and spirit of the company law. In short, every time you make a resolution, you need to draft it and have every member who agrees with it sign it the soonest. Then issue a signed copy of the draft resolution to each member of the company. That covers you so that nobody can later challenge the validity of your resolution.

Visit the IRS and fill relevant form

Now, you do not want the IRS following you on tax obligations when you are not in business. So, make it official to them that you are no longer operating as you exist in their books – the LLC that makes its annual tax returns. And you need to do that within 30 days of signing your dissolution resolution. The way to communicate this move to the IRS is by filing Form 966. After submitting that form, you can be sure you will no longer be needed to file federal tax returns.

Ensure you receive a tax certificate

Just as you don't want anyone chasing you later on unpaid debts, you don't want the state coming after you for the same reason. So, get covered by obtaining a tax certificate. This is a document that shows you have no tax obligations pending.

And you, definitely, need to pay off other debtors as well as well as collect any dues owed to the company. And then you can begin the official process of making your dissolution official.

This is the actual resolution process:

File Notice of Dissolution

Very likely, you will be required complete some standard forms. This book will not tell you if the form will be one or more, and it will not mention the length of the form(s), but the important thing is that you adhere to the requirements of the state that gave you authority to operate as an LLC. Do not lose sight of the fact that state laws can change from time to time. While you may wish to engage the services of your attorney, you also need to understand the basics of dissolution.

One document that is obvious is the General Notice of LLC Dissolution. In this one you will be required to insert:

- The name of all your members

- The business name under which you operate

- Business address

- Reference to the resolution passed by the members to dissolve the company

- Reason for company dissolution

- Name of the person authorized to receive any dues owed to the company

- Date of filing the dissolution notice

Also all members need to append their signatures to the document confirming that they concur with the notice of dissolution.

Another document that is necessary when winding up an LLC is a specific notice of dissolution to your debtors as well as creditors. In this one, what you insert is mainly:

- Name of the relevant debtor or creditor

- The name of all your members

- The business name under which you operate

- Business address

- Reference to the resolution passed by the members to dissolve the company

- Reason for company dissolution

- Name of the person authorized to receive any dues owed to the company

- Date of filing the dissolution notice

- Notice for the addressee to make any claims against the company assets, specifying the exact amount owed by the company; basis for the claim and time when claim became effective.

- Days within which the claim should be submitted – that is, from the date of the notice

- Days within which debtors should make payments – that is, from the date of the notice; name to make payments to; and the address to deliver the payments

- Stipulation that claims submitted after the deadline will be ignored

File Articles of Dissolution

- State the statute under which you are filing the articles of dissolution

- Fill in the name of your LLC

- State clearly that you have fulfilled all your financial obligations and that all dues have been paid to you

- State that the net assets have been distributed to members as per their rights and interest

- Attach a consent sheet with your company name on it, which is signed by all your members

- List also the names of your company managers and their respective addresses

- You need to have the dates written when each person signed the document

You can also have your Articles of Dissolution notarized if you deem it necessary. If you find yourself far from the offices of the Secretary of State where the relevant forms are available, you can log onto their website and download the forms. And you need to be prepared to pay a small fee for them.

It is also advisable to notify any other state office that has anything to do with the existence of your company that you have wound up your operations. A good example is the office concerned with licensing.

Chapter 12 – Why You Can Be Forced to Wind Up Your LLC

Being forced to wind up is technically known as involuntary dissolution. This means that you are going to cease operations, not out of your own volition, but due to circumstances beyond your control. One thing you need to know is that some reasons are unique to some states and so you need to learn what the law regarding the running of LLCs stipulates in your state of registration.

Matters Surrounding Involuntary Dissolution

How can your company be wound up without you making a deliberate decision to do so? Ordinarily an LLC is in perpetual existence until the people who brought it to be decide it needs to wind up. And if the LLC was established to fulfill some specific mission, then its existence extends only up to the time the mission is completed. Yet, it is possible and it does happen that an LLC is wound up without the option to consult the owners.

For instance, there are those obligations that you automatically take up once you become an LLC. One of those obligations is filing tax returns. And there may be other reports that are prescribed by the state you are operating in. Whenever you fail to fulfill any of those obligations, what you are essentially doing is abandoning the charter that the state accorded you. So the state can take whatever preliminary steps they deem fit in ensuring you adhere to the state laws, but if you prove irredeemable, the state may just have to dissolve or cancel your charter on the basis of abandonment.

However, you need to realize that you just cannot accumulate unpaid taxes and expect to get away with it through involuntary abandonment. There may be dire consequences for company directors and officials in their individual capacities before the LLC is finally forced to wind up. It is always advisable to consult your tax and legal advisors if you find your company in a tricky situation where you may come at loggerheads with the law.

Withdrawal in Foreign States

There is automatic cessation of the LLC's operations in foreign states whenever the LLC faces dissolution in its state of formation. In short, the risk of the parent company winding up puts its foreign branches at risk of winding up in whatever foreign states they are operating in. Therefore, if your LLC is involuntarily dissolved, you need to take the initiative to pay up any debts you may have accumulated in your foreign operations, make your final tax returns abroad and do the necessary paperwork to summarize your withdrawal. Just remember that each state has its own way of handling matters of official business and you should not make assumptions based on your state of residence.

Who needs to know that you are dissolving as an LLC?

Let's just admit you don't work in isolation. And so when it's time to call it quits, even when it was an inevitable move, you need to inform all the stakeholders, especially those you may owe as well as those who may owe you.

Then there are your agents, if you have any, and your vendors. They do make business commitments based on your business relationship, and so the dissolution of your LLC is bound to have an impact on their business too. As such, you need to let them know that your relationship is about to come to an end. And this is best done in writing.

Mind the law within your state of operation

The reason for this emphasis is that ignorance, as you may well know, is hardly an excuse. So business savvy as you may be, you could be brought down by just errors of omission or commission when you fail to adhere to the law governing operation and cessation of operation within the state where you are actively in business. As has been stated earlier on in this book, the things that could lead to involuntary winding up often vary from one state to another. Let's take some for example:

The State of Florida

The reasons for involuntary dissolution of an LLC in Florida include:

- Failure to file the LLC's annual report in a timely manner

- Failure to pay necessary fees within stipulated time

- Failure to update relevant state offices within 30 days of any changes that you make to information registered in those offices.

- Failure to respond to any state inquiries of a formal nature in a timely manner.

Florida Conditions of re-instatement after involuntary dissolution

It is not unusual for an LLC to wish to resume operations after it has been involuntarily dissolved. However, it has to meet certain conditions as per the laws of the state. The main ones include:

- Pay some prescribed re-instatement fee

- Pay fees accruing from non-filing of annual reports since the date of your LLC's dissolution

- File an official form for Limited Liability Re-instatement

- Obtain a filing number for your LLC documents

And you need to know that you have options in how you want to go about making your official application. You can either download the official form and then complete it and deliver it to the offices of the Division of Corporations or log onto the Department of State's website and do your filing online.

Does the filing process take long?

Well, in Florida, they try to hasten business. If you have done your filing online, the processing takes only two or three days. If you have used the post office for the delivery of your documents, then it could take a week. If you deem it urgent, the state has a provision for same-day service on request.

Is there a minimum period you need to be out of business to qualify for re-instatement?

Gladly, Florida doesn't have too many restrictions as far as resuming operations as an LLC goes. As long as you do the formal filing process and pay the requisite fees, you can have your LLC back in operation any time after the involuntary dissolution. It does not matter how recently your LLC got dissolved or long ago that was.

As you file your application for re-instatement, you can make some formal changes to suit your LLC; details varying from your initial registration. For example:

- You are allowed to change the official address on your re-instatement form; that is, your principal address for your LLC. And, of course, you can also do this on e-mail, via corpaddresschange@dos.state.fl.us

- You are also allowed to change your registered agent

- You can also take the opportunity to amend your list of members and even managers

The State of Montana

The reasons for involuntary dissolution of an LLC in Montana include:

- Failure to file the LLC's annual report with the office of the Secretary of State by the due date of December 1st. Normally, you will receive a reminder from that office and if you fail to respond to that too you are due for administrative dissolution – which in itself is involuntary dissolution.

- Failure to adhere to other statutory filings within the time stipulated. In such instances, the LLC gets listed among defaulting LLCs whose operations can be stopped within 90 days of non-compliance of the cited state regulations.

- A court decree can also lead also to involuntary dissolution of an LLC

- In times of involuntary dissolution of an LLC, company assets are left in the custody of the directors who then oversee the payment of debts and disbursement of remaining assets.

Montana Conditions of re-instatement after involuntary dissolution

Can your LLC be registered again after undergoing involuntary dissolution? The answer is yes, it can. However, there are a few things it has to do before the formalities of re-instatement can begin, namely:

Filing of Application of Re-instatement

In Montana, if the charter for your LLC were to be re-instated, then you would need to file this application of re-instatement within 5yrs of the LLC's dissolution.

Title 15 Tax Certificate

You would also need to obtain a Title 15 Tax Certificate from the state Department of Revenue, and you should submit it together with your application of re-instatement.

Update past records

You cannot get away with any reports you failed to submit in your earlier life. This means that you must, of necessity, file any annual reports you failed to submit before the involuntary dissolution of your LLC. You also need to pay up any fines or penalties levied over time for non-compliance.

Conditions of involuntary dissolution and re-instatement vary from state to state, with some aspects being common to most states. Other conditions that prevail in other US states, including Illinois, include:

- The purpose for which the LLC was incorporated becoming invalid or unsustainable

- If a member of the LLC acts in a manner that makes it difficult for the LLC to continue transacting business within the state

- Some members, officers or even directors having acted in a manner that is fraudulent, oppressive, criminal or generally illegal making the company's continued existence untenable.

- If the company wishes to engage in business other than what they indicated in their articles of organization as well as in their operating agreement, it may just have to dissolve as it cannot engage in that business as it is.

Chapter 13 – The Much You Need to Know About LLC Bankruptcy

When do you file for bankruptcy?

As an LLC, you file for bankruptcy when you cannot pay your debts as per formal agreements. The relief you get after filing for bankruptcy is that no creditor can follow you up demanding that you pay outstanding debts and so as a director or manager, your sleepless nights are over.

Another advantage is that you get a chance to meet high priority obligations first. Mind you when an LLC owes state levies or taxes, directors or company officers can be held personally liable. So it is in their interest to file for bankruptcy when taxes are in arrears because then the trustee will settle those overdue taxes and other high priority dues first, thus giving reprieve to company owners and officers.

And what is the downside to filing for bankruptcy?

Well, once you succeed in filing for bankruptcy, your position changes to one where you cannot transact official business, at least until the process of liquidation is over. So even if a lucrative deal were to come up, you cannot enter into it, as you are legally incapacitated from doing business.

Then there is the question of the value of the assets. The liquidator, who is the bankruptcy trustee, is in a hurry to get creditors paid off and complete his job. So you cannot expect your assets to fetch as much as they would if you were in charge of selling them yourself. So at the end of the day the company assets will settle a less amount of debt than would have happened if the company itself conducted the liquidation process.

Of course you also have to foot the bills for the services of the bankruptcy trustee as well as those of your attorney. The assumption here is that you engaged the services of an attorney to handle the process of filing for bankruptcy. So, clearly, while helpful in getting creditors off your back, bankruptcy also comes with extra financial costs.

In addition to those shortcomings, there is also the fact that people who partnered with you when your LLC business was still thriving and suffered or were at the verge of suffering loss when you filed for bankruptcy may be hesitant to engage with you again. This could make it difficult for you to grow your business in the same state where you operated before; the place where you have many business and personal contacts.

Does it mean you are as good as dissolved when you go bankrupt?

No, bankruptcy is not equal to dissolution. In bankruptcy, your LLC still remains the legal entity that it was initially, only that there is no room to enter into business contracts until you become liquid again; and even then, not in your current identity. After filing for bankruptcy, you need to formally apply for dissolution and follow the relevant procedures for your LLC to cease to exist as a legal entity.

The only areas that a bankrupt LLC may share with an LLC that is heading for dissolution is the priority in paying off debts and the general fact that as an individual member you are not personally liable. Once you file for bankruptcy, you are expected to allow the court trustee to dispose of some of your LLC's assets and pay off company debts to the extent possible. The reason we are speaking of 'some' of your assets being disposed of and not 'all' of them is that in some states you may be allowed to retain what is considered tools of trade so that you are able to start earning afresh and the members of the LLC do not become a liability to the state.

Of course, if you have made personal guarantees for company loans you may have to forfeit some personal property too in order to help settle any outstanding debts you have guaranteed. And if you think your state is one of those that do not leave you with any business assets, including the basics of trade, then you could dispose of them before filing for bankruptcy so that you can have some cash to replace them after the dissolution and start life anew.

How The Law of Bankruptcy Applies in The US

Once you are convinced that it may be impossible for your LLC to meet its financial obligations, you can file for bankruptcy under Chapter 7 of the Bankruptcy Code. The implication of doing this is that someone else who is not part of your organization is appointed by the court of law to undertake the role of liquidating the company assets. After filing for bankruptcy, the LLC stops transacting business and the state appointee takes over company activities.

This person, who is officially the bankruptcy trustee, sells the company assets and settles the debts that the proceeds from the assets can pay. The trustee is trusted to conduct the liquidation of assets in an orderly manner so that the assets fetch the most amount of money possible within a reasonably short period of time. The trustee also ensures that there is equity in the way the company debts are settled, even taking into account that secured creditors have an advantage over unsecured ones.

One thing you need to realize as you prepare to file for bankruptcy is that once your company has been declared bankrupt, the bankruptcy trustee can dispose of any company assets in any particular order and neither the directors and officers or any company member can interfere with the trustee's work. However, you may wish to find out in advance if your state is one of those that allow the business to retain its basic tools of trade in times of bankruptcy.

This is the position after the bankruptcy trustee is through:

- Creditors are paid to the extent the LLC's assets covered

- The LLC ceases to owe anybody, even when the outstanding debts were not paid in full.

No creditor is permitted to claim any further payment from the company thereafter; including lease owners; utility providers; issuers of credit cards; or any other business creditor.

The overall implication of filing for bankruptcy is that the company is discharged from any debt responsibility while the creditors have no option but to write off any outstanding debts. The bankruptcy trustee's job is done when he or she has forwarded any net assets to the company owners. However, truth be told, how much is there to give back if the business could not meet its obligations in the first place? In short, this is a statement that is more theoretical than real, but you need to be aware of it just in case there are some assets that were not saleable but may be of use to the company.

Why is it important to formally dissolve a bankrupt LLC?

As far as the law goes, an LLC is in existence until it is formally dissolved. The procedures for dissolution of an LLC have already been explained in earlier chapters, and as long as you have not undertaken those steps, your LLC still remains in the books of the state.

Here are the implications:

- You could be expected to file annual reports like any other LLC

- There may be minimum taxes expected from the LLC

- Your LLC may accumulate fines and penalties over the period certain obligations are not met

For these reasons, it is best to go through the procedures of dissolution to avoid getting into trouble with the law. Besides, once your LLC has been formally dissolved, hence ceasing to exist as a business entity, it becomes crystal clear to any creditors whose debts the company did not clear that the LLC is no longer in business and that its outstanding debts had better be written off as bad debts.

So, how long should you remain quiet before re-entering the business scene?

Well, you can lie low as long as you wish, but it makes sense when you are trying to allow your marred business name to escape creditors' attention. One thing you need to realize also is that if you re-open your business soon after filing for bankruptcy, the creditors whose debts you did not clear are bound to come running baying for your blood, so to speak. They will want you to meet your obligations as you had committed yourself to doing in the first place. And the courts may not manage to cover you under the chapter on bankruptcy because it will appear like your claim for bankruptcy was not sound – like it was fake; baseless; possibly motivated by cunning.

The best thing is, therefore, to take some time off, and when you do come back into business, you register a new Employer Identification Number as well as a fresh Tax Number. As an LLC, you do not receive a discharge from bankruptcy. Often what is recommended in times of bankruptcy of an LLC, particularly if you have made some personal guarantees against some company loans is to file a statement of resignation as the LLC's registered agent even before the company files for bankruptcy. That is particularly important if you have been operating as if you and the company are one and the same entity. You may then file for personal bankruptcy to deter any creditor from coming for your assets following your personal guarantee on the company loans.

Once you have filed for bankruptcy you have protection such that:

- No creditor can initiate legal proceedings against you or your company

- Nobody can lay claim over any of your personal property

- No one can create or even enforce a lien against your property

- Nobody can purport to set off any indebtedness against you until the bankruptcy process is in motion

- How to use bankruptcy to protect you

Once you file for bankruptcy as an LLC, under Chapter 7, the court appoints a trustee to oversee the disposal of company assets and settling of debts in fair proportions. Whatever extent the assets of the LLC manage to cover the debts is what company creditors can claim. Beyond that nobody can harass any of the company directors or officials,. or lay a hand on their personal property.

However, whereas you are a separate legal entity from your LLC, if there is any loan that was given to the company on the strength of your personal guarantee, then you are liable even in times of business bankruptcy to the extent of your guarantee. Still, under the law of bankruptcy, you have room to escape attachment and that is by filing for personal bankruptcy. No creditor can lay claim to your assets even if you had used them to guarantee their loans if you file for personal bankruptcy. Often, creditors who insist on personal guarantees include banks and landlords. On the overall, therefore, you are safer filing for both business bankruptcy as well as personal bankruptcy.

Conclusion

While starting your first or even your second business may seem daunting, creating a limited liability company is not as difficult as it seems. Just remember the ten steps you have to take in order to get it registered and have everything in place:

1. Figure out where you need to organize.
2. Choose a legal name.
3. Find a registered agent.
4. Hire an attorney or organize it yourself.
5. Determine your ownership status.
6. File the articles of organization with the state secretary.
7. Order the LLC Kit and Seal (Optional)
8. Choose the managers or define the management roles.
9. Prepare and approve an operating agreement.
10. Obtain the federal tax identification number.

Once you have all of that completed, then you have a company!

I hope you enjoyed the information you found in this book and found it useful. If so, please leave a review at your online eBook retailer's website.

Thank you for reading!

Made in the USA
Middletown, DE
29 September 2016